U0000028

mark

這個系列標記的是一些人、一些事件與活動。

The Calm after the Storm

A PHOTOBOOK OF TAWIAN'S JOURNEY TO MARRIAGE EQUALITY (2016-2019)

雨過天青

2016 - 2019
有你一起走的婚姻平權攝影故事書

彩虹平權大平台 Taiwan Equality Campaign
著

此書獻給合一

23,487,509 位國民，盼人人長成自己的獨特與美好，一同生活在這片多元共好的土地。

3,507,665 位選民，毋忘我們在 2018 年的公投，和平權堅毅同行，給予彼此溫暖和相挺。

559,000 位行動者，為自己所相信的價值而站出來，一同參與 8 場大型街頭行動。

16,895 位台灣的自主公民，感謝支持婚姻平權大平台發起的 3 場群眾募資捐款方案，讓全世界看見台灣民主、自由、進步的公民社會。

陪伴大平台一路走來、海內外的志工夥伴、小蜜蜂與小可愛們。

特別獻給畢安生老師及親友，以及多多巫緒樑，你們留下的愛與勇氣，引領台灣走向更好的改變。

特別感謝—

祁家威、童子賢、王小棣、鄭弘儀、蔣承縉（蔣哥）、林大涵與貝殼放大、
最強後盾馬桶、封面人物魏嫵琇

Freedom to Marry Global ｜ Evan Wolfson, Thalia Zepatos, Cameron Tolle
Open Society Foundations ｜ Michael Haflin, Joy Chia
Equality Without Borders ｜ Julie Dorf, Bill Smith, Chris Cordingles
Yes Equality Australia ｜ Alex Greenwich, Tom Snow, Adam Knobel, Tim Gartrell
Human Rights Campaign ｜ Global Team
OurRight Action International ｜ Jessica Stern

曾於婚姻平權大平台與
現於彩虹平權大平台或合作過的—

團體

台灣同志諮詢熱線協會、台灣同志家庭權益促進會、婦女新知基金會、同志人權法案遊說聯盟、GagaOOLala 同志影音平台、基本書坊、同志同光長老教會、真光福音教會、台灣性別平等教育協會、台中基地、台南新芽、高雄市女權會、性平教育大平台、平權公投團隊，與 68 組全台公投協力團體、給力夥伴們。

工作夥伴

呂欣潔、鄧筑媛、Aki YJ Chen、Kelvin Lin、曹承羲、薛舜文、郭宜婷、黃馨儀、林忠毅、王祥、林鈺婷、翁鈺清、任紋潔、李芝晨、劉宇霆、馮梅君、周芷萱、李屏瑤、張瓊文、李政翰、鄭昱菁、陳玉珂、吳東穎、黃譯萱、林風吟、陳乃嘉、忻儀、林均諺、卓芸萱、姚皖萱、潘乃亘（以加入時序排列）

理監事

李屏瑤、鄒宗翰、蘇珊、彭治鏐、陳盈蓁、黎璿萍、杜思誠、Ciwang · Teyra、 鄧傑、李政翰、林貫方、林志杰

2 0 1

3

民進黨立委尤美女與數個國內性別、同志組織、法界人士等共同組成「同婚修法小組」，定期討論民法修正方向及內容。

5.17

「同性婚姻收養子女課題座談會」，由尤美女委員辦公室舉辦，廣邀同志社群進行內部座談。

8

同婚草案初步完成，同志及性別團體與尤美女立委辦公室至高雄、台南、台中、桃園等地徵詢社群意見。

10.16

畢安生（Jacques Picoux）老師辭世，引發輿論關注同志伴侶權益。

10.24

同志及性別團體與尤美女立委合作之「民法親屬編修正草案」召開記者會宣告提出草案。同日，時代力量黨團亦提出黨團版本「民法親屬編修正草案」。

10.25

許毓仁立法委員提案「民法親屬編修正草案」。

10.26

同志及性別團體召開「同志家庭不能等，婚姻平權要全面」聯合記者會。

11.7

同志父母共同召開「一群擔憂的家長，別讓我們的孩子無法成家」聯合記者會。

11.8

尤美女立委及許毓仁立委提案「民法親屬編修正草案」皆一讀通過。

11.10

大平台召開「異性戀家長支持婚姻平權，愛是平等，不分性別」聯合記者會。

11.11

時代力量黨團提案「民法親屬編修正草案」一讀通過。

11.17

尤美女立委任司法及法制委員會召集委員，排審民法親屬編修正案。反同團體聚集於濟南路反對修法，於壓力下司法法制委員會決議加開兩場公聽會。

11.24

第九屆立法院司法及法制委員會第一次婚姻平權公聽會。

11.28

「相挺為平權，全民撐同志」

📍 台灣婚姻平權修法第二場公聽會，青島東路上

2016 年冬日，婚姻平權議題成了社會上的話題焦點，「直接修民法」及「另立專法」兩派產生激辯。11 月 28 日，立法院司法及法制委員會針對婚姻平權修法召開第二場公聽會，各界都到場發言，上萬名支持修民法的群眾則在立法院場外，表達對於專法的強烈反對。永遠不會忘記，那天在公聽會上，音樂人焦安溥溫柔而堅定地引用美國聯邦最高法院判決說法：「雖然法律難以改變人們的偏見，但是法律不可以為偏見服務，更不可以使人們的偏見因法律直接或間接地產生力量，」

12.3

「法律白話文運動」與「彩虹巴士陣線」
皆發動線上募資，前者於四大報刊登
「法律不該為偏見服務、讓愛平權」之
廣告，後者包車北上參與 12.10 音樂會。

12.5

為籌措法案遊說、倡議資金，發起「全
民挺同婚，現正募資中！」群眾募資，
三天內募得一千萬。

12.10

「讓生命不再逝去，為婚姻平權站出來」音樂會

📍 凱達格蘭大道上

2016 年世界人權日，我們在凱道上，站出來為自己與身旁的人發聲。就在前一週，反
同團體發起遊行，在凱道高呼「婚姻家庭，全民決定」，充滿歧視意味的口號，對同
志朋友來說心仿如刀割；隔週，超過 25 萬人在相同地點聚首，響應「讓生命不再逝去，
為婚姻平權站出來」音樂會，從白天到黑夜，揮舞著「SEE MY RIGHTS NOW!」旗幟，
為平權發聲。那天，包含陳珊妮、何韻詩、戴愛玲、HUSH 等 25 組音樂人接力演唱；
而張惠妹、蔡依林、蕭亞軒等天后級巨星也透過影片相挺。溫暖的歌聲下，凱道上飄
揚著無數彩虹旗。那個又哭又笑的夜晚，我們因為彼此的相伴，知道自己其實不孤單。

12.26

「爭取婚姻平權，用愛守護立院」

📍 第九屆立法院司法及法制委員會第二次婚姻平權法案審查，濟南路上

經過公聽會及正反兩方動員表達訴求，當年 12 月 26 日是立法院首度逐條審查婚姻平權法案。場外挺同、反同陣營各據一方，高喊訴求的同時，也為國會裡頭的審查結果焦急著。在場內激烈的言詞交鋒、場外高漲的對立聲浪中，朝野雙方達成共識，通過了一個融合各方意見，最能為社會所接受的跨黨派版本。這是台灣首次有於《民法》增列同性婚姻的草案送出委員會。聽到這個消息的那一刻，同志族群長久得不到回應的微弱盼望，好像終於露出了一點點光。

2 0 1

1.15

召開平權紅包袋記者會，邀請民眾索取平權紅包袋，回家過年包給家人，同時開啟對話。

1.25

刊登「希望下個過年，我們一起回家吃年夜飯」報紙廣告。

2.10

司法院公布受理祁家威、台北市政府釋憲聲請，宣布將於 3 月 24 日召開憲法法庭審理此案。

2.18

總統府邀請同志伴侶與家庭會見蔡英文總統、陳建仁副總統等政府官員。

3.3

Facebook 發起「『同志生命故事，未完成的權利清單』一人一故事，寫給大法官」活動。

3.11

與婚姻平權小蜜蜂一起發送「白色情人節，彩虹甜在心」喜糖，向路人傳遞愛和同志伴侶想成家的心願。

3.15

舉辦「立法釋憲的必勝之路，大法官幫幫忙！」講座，由婦女新知基金會林實芳律師、民間司法改革基金會周宇修律師北中南同時開講。

3.16

召開「一人一故事，寫給大法官」募集同志生命未完成的權利清單記者會，將募集的生命故事擬成法庭之友意見書，寄送給大法官。

3.20

民間團體舉辦「性別教育，終止霸凌，給孩子更有希望的未來」聯合記者會，呼籲執政者與釋憲者，看到性別平等環境與教育對於孩子的影響。

3.22

· 包含精神醫學、心理、法律、社工、教育、政治、性別研究、公衛等領域專家、學者主筆撰寫，綜合同志真實生命故事而成的 14 份法庭之友意見書全數上網公布，並寄送給大法官。

· 發起「2017 有愛一同、修民法讓人人能合法結婚」跨界名人一起舉牌支持婚姻平權。

3.24

祁家威與台北市政府兩案之聲請釋憲案，大法官召開憲法法庭。前者委任台灣伴侶權益推動聯盟的許秀雯律師、莊喬汝律師、潘天慶律師，以及北市府由政大法律系廖元豪教授為代理人。

3.26

「大甲媽祖，彩虹接駕」於彰化員林設香案，迎大甲媽祖遶境。媽祖鑾駕於案前落轎，將鑾轎壓過的壓轎金發送遶境民眾，盼邀請傳統信仰信眾，一同了解同志成家故事。

4.10

與婚姻平權小蜜蜂一同於小學門口發送兒童節貼紙，透過機會和家長溝通性別平等教育。

4.23

與微光計畫共同舉辦「萌萌大解密」歐陽文風牧師巡迴講座。

4.24

司法院大法官發布新聞稿，表示將於 5 月 24 日公布同婚釋憲案結果。

4.27

舉辦「婚姻平權通過後，那些國家怎麼了？」加法英美各國經驗分享座談會，各國在通過同志婚姻之後並未因此加深恐慌，而是在過程中深化民主與人權價值。

5.1

與女書店合作於 Facebook 發起「自己的立委自己教！打造地方性別小書庫」，捐款送書給立委的活動。

5.5

舉辦法庭之友系列講座「歧視有病！還是同志有病？」，邀請主筆法庭之友意見書之一的徐志雲醫師，分享十招破除萌萌的偽精神醫學。

5.10

發起「相愛不分異同之媽媽我想對你說」網路母親節活動，讓社會看見同志與家人的動人故事。

5.24

「點亮台灣，亞洲燈塔」　婚姻平權再戰立院

📍 大法官釋憲結果公布，青島東路上

那天下午，大法官做出《釋字第 748 號解釋》，宣布現行《民法》未保障同性婚姻自由有違憲法，應在二年之內修正或制定相關法案；總統府也敦促行政部門盡速修法，呼籲社會以理解、包容、尊重的態度，面對與自己意見不同的人。這個釋憲案起源於台灣同志運動先鋒者祁家威、和三對女同志伴侶，於 2013 年、2014 年到戶政事務所登記結婚遭拒絕，而後祁家威提起訴願、行政訴訟皆失敗，最後再聲請大法官釋憲；台北市政府也主張民法規定違憲，提起釋憲聲請。最後大法官在解釋理由書中，也寫出早在 1986 年，祁家威就召開記者會爭取同性婚姻，期間同志們陸續挺身而出。為了這一天，同志們一起等了超過三十年。

5.26

釋憲後，大平台隨即召開「平權之光，點亮台灣」記者會，宣布發起「平權之光，全台發亮」活動，要求行政院盡速修法、檢討相關法規。

5.31

立法院司法及法制委員會召集委員尤美女召集民法修正草案協商會議。

6.7

釋憲後，行政院組成同婚修法專案小組並召開第一次會議，決議先檢討現行行政法規，對同性配偶規定放寬。

6.14

行政院召開同婚修法專案小組第二次會議，檢視民法相關規定，認為結婚年齡與夫妻財產制等同性配偶均可適用現行民法規定。

6.21

行政院召開同婚修法專案小組第三次會議，內政部啟動跨區同性伴侶註記，檢討民法親屬編婚姻普通效力條文，同性配偶均可適用。

7.6

「婚姻自由之平等保障」判決之後台美大對談」邀請法學者張宏誠、美國推動婚權的 Evan Wolfson 律師對談美國聯邦最高法院判決與台灣大法官釋憲。

8.3

發起網路活動「讓愛成家，我愛爸爸」，邀請同志網友訴說與爸爸的感人故事。

8.9

釋憲後，台北高等行政法院首度就同婚登記案開庭審理，大平台發出新聞稿，呼籲行政院盡速提出修正法案。

8.22

「愛情故事館：許我們一個未來」展覽台北開展，讓同志伴侶與青少年的故事呈現在眾人面前，希望邀請更多人站出來支持。

8.23

呂欣潔、陳凌同性婚姻登記行政訴訟案開庭，開庭後當事人與律師於法庭外召開記者會。

9.29

召開「不要再有下一個畢安生，婚姻平權就是現在！」記者會，宣布將舉辦畢安生紀念晚會，也邀請到酷兒盟秘書長胡勝翔現身說法，要求政府立即修法保障他與伴侶的權益。

10.3

行政院院長賴清德接受柯志恩立法委員質詢時表示，預算會期提出修法有困難，婚姻平權大平台發出「新科行政院長拖延修法？民進黨應即刻兌現選前政見！」聲明，要求立刻修法，不要再有下一個畢安生。

10.12

釋憲後，行政法院首度對於同婚登記被拒案做成判決，戶政拒絕同性別者登記結婚處分違法撤銷，但亦駁回當事人要求法院命戶政機關為結婚登記的訴求。

10.6

賴清德院長於立院接受許毓仁立法委員質詢時表示，不放棄於 2017 年提出草案。

10.13

祁家威因投身同志運動、推動婚姻平權，提起釋憲案，榮獲總統文化獎之社會改革獎。

10.16

畢安生老師逝世一週年，為紀念畢老師對於台灣的貢獻，卻因法律上欠缺對同性婚姻的保障而留下遺憾，於凱達格蘭大道舉辦「再也等不到，我們都是畢安生」紀念晚會。

10.28

大平台參加台灣同志遊行，擔任綠色大隊頭車，帶領群眾發起教育部前「再見玫瑰少年」與「拒絕等待、終止遺憾血手印」快閃活動。

11.17

「愛情故事館：許我們一個未來」展覽於高雄駁二開展。

2 0 1

1.26

於行政院前大樓（中山北路與忠孝東路口）放置「平等成家，還要等多久？」大型廣告看板，要求行政院加快修法腳步。

2

下一代幸福聯盟發起反對以民法讓同志結婚，與反對同志教育進入校園的公投提案。

2.9

前往都柏林拜訪愛爾蘭公投團隊，為即將發生的公投戰做萬全的準備。

3.31

舉辦「性別公民站出來，爸爸媽媽一起來」婚姻平權地方遊說培力工作坊。

5.10

舉辦「對話志工」第一次線上培訓。

5.15

召開「家家好家，有愛成家」2018 年台北市同志公民活動記者會。

5.16

舉辦「粉紅經濟起飛，台灣準備好了嗎？」2018 年國際家庭日系列文化講座啟動，分別就「粉紅經濟」、「以設計做運動」方向進行討論。

5.17

開啟「蜂潮行動，飛越同溫層」募資計畫，召開「2018 反恐同恐跨恐雙日，大平台邀你用對話為愛找捷徑」記者會。

5.24

舉辦「家家好家，有愛成家」2018 年國際家庭日草地園遊會，邀請超過五十組友善商家、藝人表演，華山大草坪充滿各種多元家庭的身影，已故香港藝人盧凱彤當時亦獻唱支持。

5.25

舉辦「婚姻平權，平等成家？」國際修法論壇，邀請荷蘭、法國、澳洲率先提出婚姻平權法案的國會議員們來台，分享不同國家的修法過程與策略，同時拜會總統府、立法院，提醒他們加快腳步。

6.11

「台灣社會質化研究：焦點訪談執行」各地開跑，是台灣首次針對同志議題的社會態度調查。

7.23

美澳公投顧問團隊來台培訓工作坊，傳授面對公投的準備。

7.27

與高雄哲學星期五團隊共同舉辦「大法官釋憲 vs. 反同婚公投 — 直接民主的理想與現實」講座。

8.29

召開「三個不同意，幸福ＯＫ！」募集百萬不同意票行動正式開跑記者會。

8.30

下一代幸福聯盟所提出的「民法婚姻限定一男一女」、「國中小禁止實施同志教育」以及「民法婚姻以外形式保障同性伴侶」三案已完成第二階段連署送件中央選舉委員會。

9.4

婚姻平權公投推動小組向中央選舉委員會送交「婚姻平權」、「確立性別平等教育」兩案二階段 47 萬份連署書，最終認定 43 萬份有效。

9.11

「名人來 Call Out」首波直播上線，每週邀請一位名人打電話給身邊的朋友，傳授如何進行溝通對話，並提供公投最新消息。

9.21

舉辦「釋憲之後，修法之前！公投元年的婚姻平權」哲學星期五講座。

9.24

呂欣潔前往泰國分享婚權公投挑戰，為台灣首位受邀至泰國外國記協演講。

9.25

發布跨團體（婚姻平權大平台、台灣伴侶權益推動聯盟、平權前夕‧彩虹起義、性別平等教育大平台）聯合聲明，共同推出「1124 返家投票，兩好三壞，投出台灣幸福未來」行動。

10.4

發布「2018公投元年，友善候選人」名單並召開候選人友善意向調查記者會。

10.9

下一代幸福聯盟所提出的「民法婚姻限定一男一女」、「國中小禁止實施同志教育」、「民法婚姻以外形式保障同性伴侶」，中選會宣布成案。

10.11

中央選舉委員會宣布,「婚姻平權」、「確立性別平等教育」兩案跨越連署門檻,並於 10 月 16 日審議通過。

10.13

公投成案後,為讓各地民眾了解公投議題,並傳授對話技巧,婚姻平權大平台與全台各地方組織、團體、學校、友善店家,合作舉辦公投說明會、培訓,一個月內舉辦超過 20 場。

10.14

「愛情故事館:許我們一個未來」於桃園光影展出,持續讓同志生命被看見。

10.17

「彩虹 V 計畫」由伴侶盟、愛最大共同發起,大平台和平權公投小組共同聲援,盼團結創造更多改變。

10.19

「加入插旗點,相挺幸福未來」全台插旗點計畫正式上線,一千幅橫旗一週內就被索取完畢。

10.27

大平台以「兩好三壞公投練習賽」為主題參加台灣同志遊行,教育民眾如何投票。

10.31

「非常召集——牽手步入禮堂的最後一哩路」群眾集資計畫開跑,一週募得一千萬的廣告資金,使用於最後一個月的車體與電視、報紙廣告購買。

11.2

召開「謠言滿天飛,我們來終結!」破除反同團體十大謊言記者會。

11.2

台灣鄉親與美國同婚團體 Freedom to Marry 於美國紐約石牆酒吧共同舉辦「Love from Stonewall - Support Marriage Equality in Taiwan」公投說明會

11.23

展開「回家吧!全台車站接人計畫」,多位藝人共襄盛舉,在家鄉車站一同迎接遊子回鄉投票。

11.18

「為愛返家,搭上幸福特快車」
兩好三壞音樂會

📍 凱達格蘭大道上

2018 年底,九合一縣市長選舉即將登場,在宗教反同團體搶先連署提案之下,發起針對同性婚姻、性別平等教育等多項議題進行公投,其中一案「你是否同意以民法婚姻規定以外之其他形式來保障同性別二人經營永久共同生活的權益?」便是衝著婚姻平權而來;眼見反同團體就釋憲結果訴諸公投作為策略反制,苗博雅等人亦發起平權公投。這場公投對決,儘管同志社群與社會面臨諸多拉鋸、撕扯,我們也只能竭盡所能串聯與動員,用盡全力打贏這輪不得的一役。投票日前一週,婚姻平權大平台與平權公投小組在凱達格蘭大道舉辦「為愛返家,搭上幸福特快車」音樂會,以「兩好三壞」為口號,邀請民眾返家對反同三案投下三個不同意票,並對平權兩案投下兩個同意票。

11.24

開票之夜

2018 年 11 月 24 日,首次與反同團體正面交鋒,耗費大量資源動員的公投結果不如人意,反同團體提出的同婚不修民法、另立專法、反對同志教育等訴求大獲全勝,三案全數壓倒性通過門檻,而同志團體提出的平權兩案則皆慘遭否決。這也意味著政府將依據公投結果,在三個月內提出保障同婚的專法。那個寒冷而漆黑的夜,無數挺同夥伴與同志朋友都傷透了心,甚而有輕生念頭,眾多團體一直以來的努力好似轉瞬成了泡影,對許多同志來說,彷彿連存在在世界上的意義都連同公投結果遭到否定。那天晚上,台灣同志權益最黑暗的一夜,我們的心都碎了,連呼吸都覺得困難,只能用剩下最後一點點力氣相信,平權或許仍有到來的一天。

2 0 1

1.16

召開「期待蘇貞昌院長堅守 748 的憲法防線：『婚姻』才是符合憲法及實際需求的同婚法案」記者會。

1.23

發布「公投元年後的下一步：關注同婚法案，深耕彩虹台灣」聲明稿。

1.31

展開「支持你的同志親友，八大要點停看聽」網路聲援。

2.11

網路動員「情人節快樂，同志要合憲的婚姻！一起到立委的社群平台留言」行動。

2.20

蘇貞昌院長發布影片邀請國人一同讓台灣成為「互相尊重、彼此友善」的國家，並分享自身轉變經驗。團體們回應「期待同婚法案合憲且平等，建立和諧尊重的多元社會」聲明稿，並開啟網路動員，支持合憲同婚專法之行動。

2.21

行政院會通過《司法院釋字第 748 號解釋施行法》草案（後稱同婚專法），送往立法院等待審議。團體們共同發布「婚姻平權大平台針對行政院版草案三點聲明」聲明稿。

3.5

同婚專法草案通過一讀。大平台發布「盼立院大步前行，用圓滿成家取代社會爭議」回應《司法院釋字 748 號施行法》通過院會一讀之聲明稿。

3.12

國民黨賴士葆委員提出《公投第 12 案施行法》（為同性共同生活法），網路動員「要求撤簽草案」行動。

3.14

大平台支援台灣同志家庭權益促進會舉辦「請賴士葆委員撤回提案，讓同志家庭融入台灣社會」記者會，要求賴士葆儘速撤簽草案。

3.15

大平台發布「呼籲各黨立委莫支持違憲法案，盡速完成大法官交付之同婚修法」回應《公投第 12 案施行法》通過院會一讀之聲明稿。

3.16

「逆風飛行：彩虹樁腳工作坊」政治遊說志工招募培訓全台開跑。

4.2

網路動員「連假動起來！要求委員支持行政院版本同婚法案」行動。

4.15

展開「讓 524 個祝福 +1」線上募集祝福留言行動。

4.19

發布「修民法當兒戲？反同團體請勿挾持國會蔑視憲法」聲明稿。

4.24

發布「婚姻平權促進經濟成長，23 間企業期許多元共融帶台灣走向世界」聲明稿，為台灣首次募集多所跨國企業共同為婚姻平權發聲。

4.30

召開「婚姻不要一國兩制，守護子女最佳利益」聯合記者會。

5.2

民進黨立委林岱樺提出《司法院釋字第 748 號解釋暨公投第 12 案施行法》草案傳出將逕付二讀，內有家人可主張同性關係無效之條文，歧視具現。團體們因而共同發布「同志家庭退無可退，請立委支持合憲法案」聲明稿。

5.6

發布「50 家第一線婚禮產業集結祝福同志新人」新聞稿。

5.8

超過 40 組同志家庭於立院前，召開「共同監護權不穩固，孩童權益全被罔顧」聯合記者會。

5.16

發起「517 一個不能少」街頭快閃行動。

5.14

「立院協商，協商不能退！」

📍婚權緊急動員令，青島東路上

婚姻平權長路漫漫，先經歷保障同性婚姻的大法官解釋，再捱過只能走另立專法一途的公投大敗結果，《釋字 748 號》所定的兩年期限終於將至。2019 年 5 月 14 日，趕在期限之前，立法院針對同性結合、同性伴侶、與同性婚姻專法草案進行逐條朝野協商。在婚姻平權大平台緊急動員下，數千位挺同支持者擦乾眼淚、拾起破碎的心，再度回到議場外的青島東路上，高呼「結合不是結婚，台灣婚姻不要一國兩制」，呼籲支持婚姻平權的立委「協商不能退」，行政院提出的《司法院釋字第 748 號解釋施行法》專法草案已是折衷後的底線。我們都不知道結果會如何，只盼著，這一次，我們可不可以不要再傷心了。

5.17

「最後表決，表決不能輸！」

📍 婚權緊急動員令，青島東路上

朝野協商的三天後，《司法院釋字 748 號解釋施行法》送立法院院會三讀，場內朝野各黨皆動員備戰，超過三萬名支持婚姻平權的群眾則再度聚集青島東路上，一同見證這歷史性的一刻。歷經超過四個小時的逐條表決後，立法院長蘇嘉全在下午 3 點 27 分敲下議事槌，宣告《司法院釋字第 748 號解釋施行法》三讀通過，台灣也正式成為亞洲第一個同性婚姻合法化的國家。當明定「同志伴侶可向戶政機關辦理結婚登記」的第 4 條條文以多數通過，現場瞬間爆出如雷歡呼，許多人更相擁彼此，喜極而泣──那是好多好多同志數不清日子的等待，一輩子的期盼。在這年的「國際不再恐同日」5 月 17 日，台灣寫下歷史，終於，同志也可以結婚了。

5.24

「524 個祝福 +1」同志聯合婚禮

📍 台北、高雄戶政事務所

2019 年 5 月 24 日，《司法院釋字第 748 號解釋施行法》正式生效，同志伴侶從今開始，可以到戶政事務所依據該專法辦理結婚登記。當天一早，同志情侶小銘、小玄身著粉紅色西裝情侶裝，現身台北市信義區戶政事務所搶頭香登記。登記前，他們在眾人見證下甜蜜接吻，並在 8 時 38 分完成登記手續；而倡議同志權益多年的祁家威亦到場祝賀。在這特別的一天，婚姻平權大平台在信義廣場舉辦派對，多對同志新人在親友祝福下牽手進場，不少亦開心得紅了眼眶，場面歡欣而感人。那天，在台灣各個角落，許多夫夫、妻妻都在苦等已久的這一天成婚，許下攜手偕老的約定。

目次 Contents

推薦序

願陽光的溫暖始終在

《司法院釋字第748號解釋文施行法》，寫著婚姻自由、人人平等的憲法權利，有著同志朋友一路走來的掙扎與血淚，字裡行間更有社會衝突與政治爭議的妥協痕跡。

2019年5月17日，這部法通過了，象徵台灣終於跨越了歧視的社會鴻溝，跨進了一個多元包容的新時代。

就像每個新舊時代的轉移，從來不是一蹴可及；每個價值觀念的改變，也都來自於無數人的涓滴意念。這本書正記錄了許多或將在歷史長河裡被遺忘的故事，但一起走過的人會記得彼此的挫折、憤怒，以及溫暖與勇氣。

做為提出這部法案的行政院首長而言，這部法代表了行政院的態度，我有責任也有義務要讓這部法在立法院通過。但這不是件容易的事，尤其是牽涉價值的選擇、根深柢固的後天觀念，說服、溝通、折衝都是免不了的過程，理解和耐心更是必須，在法案沒通過前，我承認我也抱著忐忑的心情。但終究，這一天，多數的委員面對失去選票的恫嚇威脅，仍然選擇了站在追求人人平等的這一方。

現在回頭看，也許雲淡風輕，但當時卻是殘酷的掙扎，事後有人回憶說，每按下一次表決鍵，就像是自己往自己身上插了一把刀，看見選票不斷的流失，但這一次，多數人勇敢的守著不退，讓台灣社會往前跨了一大步。

5 月 17 日之後，生活和工作一切如常，每天依舊是亟待解決的繁重政務，一個會議接著一個會議，一個行程接著一個行程。但有一天，一個老朋友來拜會我，說有私事想和我單獨談，我略感詫異，但還是讓陪同會面的其他人迴避。偌大的會客室只剩我倆，這位朋友慎重的站定，向我深深鞠了一躬，起身後眼眶泛淚。驚訝之下，他對我說，他的女兒就是同志，多年來是家庭的痛，對女兒遭受的歧視與折磨，既疼惜又不捨。現在終於法通過了，同志可以正大光明的結婚了，他要感謝我做的努力。

那一刻，我才深刻的瞭解到，許多人和我一樣，為同志朋友發聲，讓同志可以結婚，堅持的是一種素樸的自由、平等理念，因為沒有誰有權利歧視誰；但對那些長年備受歧視、不被公平對待的同志以及親人而言，這不是理念之爭，而是每一天的生活，是每一天切身感受的痛苦，而這生活裡的痛，其實一直存在於我們的身邊，我們卻渾然不知。

生活一直走，雨過天會青，會有陽光照下來，但願這生活裡的陽光，照亮那我們忽略太久、陰暗太久的角落，讓溫暖始終在。

行政院院長
蘇貞昌

推薦序

婚姻平權的一小步，台灣人權進步的一大步

性別平等是世界人權宣言的重要目標，也是台灣社會共同努力的目標。

多年來面對同志在社會上所受的不公平待遇而致常常必需隱藏自我，我深感遺憾與自省。因此我一直主張：台灣同婚平權，也是台灣進步人權。

同婚立法一定要成功，才會帶給社會新和諧、新進步面貌，我眼中的青澀台灣才能轉型成成熟台灣，更好的開朗的進步的公民社會，這是我們應該努力追求的新面貌。而同婚立法也不會妨礙任何社會既存異性婚姻的幸福快樂。

從 2019 年 5 月 14 日到 5 月 17 日，當我們把同婚立法推進到最後關鍵的倒數階段，令人緊張、期待、興奮。當立法院蘇院長主持朝野協商，進行不同版本三個法案辯論，並逐條討論通過的緊張時刻，我自己也在青島東路上，與上萬群眾一起靜坐。而這立法院旁的小小馬路，成千上百的彩虹旗飄揚，愈來愈多的熱心市民湧入。看著來自四面八方湧入的熱血朋友，看著義工揮汗如雨，聽著廣場擴大器不斷宣佈法條的協商進度，我知道這是歷史性的一刻。

現場不斷傳出鼓掌、唱歌、喊加油聲！

我深深為台灣社會的學習與進步感動與驕傲。我對於台灣公民與輿論能透過辯論、思考、再辯論、再思考，而達成這樣的成就而驕傲。

社會不是沒有缺點，社會尚待努力改正的議題，在政治、經濟、法規上，猶待改善的還很多……在外籍移工、獨居老人、所得貧困、受虐兒童、短期契約工、流浪動物等議題上，陽光照不到的角落還很多。

但是我們從同婚法案立法開始，已踏出勇敢的一步，讓性平在家庭中在社會上得到法律的保障，這是重要的關鍵一步。讓我們再次說，留下見證不要忘記 2019 這歷史關鍵的一刻：婚姻平權的一小步，台灣人權進步的一大步。我們為自己為台灣贏得值得期待的明天。

和碩聯合科技董事長
童子賢

* Please turn to page 210 for English version

推薦序

一場帶來希望的運動

台灣在逆境與不確定中邁向婚姻平權的旅程，為全世界倡議同志社群與家庭人權的工作者們帶來了希望。這場激勵人心的運動建立了社會大眾的支持、在法律層面上提出挑戰、利用公投捍衛社群權益，並且贏得台灣政治人物在情感與理性上的認同。

台灣所遭遇的挑戰和澳洲與美國相似，這兩個國家都很榮幸得以為台灣傑出的同運工作者提供支持與鼓勵，讓他們開創新的局面，使婚姻平權在第一個亞洲國家獲得落實。

婚姻平權在台灣正式入法的這天（2019年 5 月 24 日）是一個值得歡慶的日子。在迎來這一天前，堅定投身於此議題的倡議工作者和志工經歷了多年來各種令人情緒激盪又耗費心神的收穫與失落，而如今他們將可以分享自身的成功經驗，為未來的運動提供幫助。

我們必須盡力在許多其他國家推廣婚姻自由，而台灣、亞洲和世界其他角落也依舊面臨許多挑戰。這場運動的勝利將有助於幫其他國家打下基石，並再次肯定宣告，同志屬於每個家庭、職場、宗教、社群和國家的一份子，並應該要受到法律平等和公平的對待。

在個人層面上，我想要感謝台灣的婚姻平權運動和澳洲與全球的倡議者一同合作。我們從台灣的旅程中學到許多，而台灣也將繼續激勵我們實現更多目標，並協助其他運動者在全球各處倡議公平與平等。

澳洲婚姻平權協會（Australian Marriage Equality）理事長
澳洲新南威爾斯州（NSW）議會雪梨市議員
Alex Greenwich

推薦序

愛在台灣的勝利

台灣最高法院於 2017 年 5 月的釋憲結果肯定了婚姻自由，也為接下來同志平權漫長曲折的奮戰揭開序幕——從憲法法庭、到公投票箱，又回到了立法院。這兩年，代表著反同方有充足的時間試圖阻礙婚姻平權。

婚姻平權大平台深知，為了讓台灣成為第一個贏得婚姻自由的亞洲國家，團隊要打造一場堅實的全國性運動，一場動員政治決策者、並把同性伴侶故事帶到台灣民眾眼前的運動。這領悟反映了我們（美國推動婚姻平權的團隊「Freedom to Marry」）幾個世代掙扎中所學到的教訓：安撫這類恐懼最好的方式，是訴說渴望結婚的同性伴侶們與親友互相支持的故事。

當台灣反同方強行將婚姻平權推向一場全國性公投，儘管我們相信，家庭的尊嚴不應以此決定，但藉由公投，我們的對手不經意地在台灣史上開啟了一場針對同志的大型對話，讓運動者去建立一個立基在台灣家庭、扎根於在地價值的大型草根運動。婚姻平權大平台成為全球所見過最令人驚豔的大型婚權運動之一。

大平台四處尋找台灣民眾表露自己支持婚姻平權的心聲。從 90 歲阿嬤、父親支持同志女兒的轉變旅程，到已在一起超過三十年的男同志伴侶，這些故事透過各種媒體在全台廣泛傳播，同時對每一個台灣人昭示，婚姻平權不只與同志有關，更與台灣價值有關。

2019 年 5 月，台灣取得了亞洲在婚姻自由上的首次勝利，引起全球歡慶。隨著這場勝利持續融入日常生活，如今有 60% 的台灣民眾支持婚姻平權，這證明了，當我們移除激烈言詞和恐嚇策略，讓人們看到真實已婚伴侶，多數人都能理解，結婚的同性伴侶並不會影響自己的生活，事實上還可能讓國家變得更強大。

在未來許多年間，我們都會感受到台灣的歷史性勝利所帶來的長遠影響——在亞洲的同志運動中，更在那些彼此許諾的同性伴侶的生活中。

美國推動婚權組織 Freedom to Marry

Evan Wolfson, Thalia Zepatos, Cameron Tolle

序

雨過天青

那段時間我們總在街頭相見——大型集會、街頭記者會、遊行、戶外抗議行動，在一些很重要的時刻，雨水也澆不熄我們的決心。

2016 年 12 月 10 日，25 萬人集結在凱道前，是太陽花運動後台灣最大的街頭集會，「為婚姻平權站出來」音樂會，三十幾位藝人連番上陣，經費不足又沒有足夠經驗的「同運團體」們，讓好幾位妝容精緻的女藝人淋著大雨表演，到最後，台下十幾萬人卻也都沒有離開。

2019 年 5 月 17 日那天，立法院內正在進行最後的法案投票，在雨中，我們見證著同婚法案一條一條的表決著，雨下得之大，分不清楚我們臉上的是雨水還是淚水，在拍板定案那刻，天空從雲層中露出了陽光，彩虹出現在眾人的頭頂上，雨水和淚水都被陽光曬乾，撥雲見日大概就是這種感覺，而我們都破涕為笑，不敢相信台灣社會在我們的有生之年，在我們的眼前，走到這一步。

從 2019 年 5 月 24 日那天起，台灣成為了亞洲第一個同性可以結婚的國家，至今已有超過 6000 對同性配偶在這塊土地上締結婚姻、組成國家所認可的合法家庭，甚至有不少人也透過海外人工生殖的協助，擁有了孩子。在這個社會中，人與人之間的互動和組成是個大型的有機體，當同志成為了這個國家能夠合法進入婚姻制度的一員，許多不同的故事也開始在各個角落發生、在不同的社群中產生改變的契機，而我們的下一代，將會迎來將平權與更多元的故事深植內心的未來。正因如此，我們希望在一切變得理所當然之前，記錄下這看似不可能的改變。

這是一場扎扎實實要聚集眾人之力才能合作實現的運動，三十年來台灣社會和同志社群的起伏與挑戰，絕非用三言兩語能夠呈現，此書嘗試從大平台的角度出發，將 2016-2019 這三年多來的日子所經歷的點滴用影像與文字稍加紀錄下來，近四年是不短的日子，紙短情長，要說的故事太多，或不夠完整，只盼我們都能記得這段共同努力的、前所未有又難以被遺忘的歷史。

這本攝影故事書是獻給每一位為婚姻平權運動付出的人，不只是在台灣的你們、也有在世界各地的好多好多夥伴們：不只是現在的我們，更有過去的每一份努力與血淚。我也想藉此機會，感謝支持大平台的朋友，以及所有過去與現在參與在大平台工作中的夥伴，我們挑戰了作為運動者在意志與體力的極限、人跟人與團體之間合作的極限、以及學習了如何放下自我意識邁向共好，為同一個目標共同前行尋找前進的方法，或許過程並不全然的美好，但相信在我們的生命中都是重要的學習。

未來平權之路仍顛簸，但有眾人之力，改變一定會發生！

彩虹平權大平台執行長

呂欣潔

概論

INTRODUCTION

彩虹平權大平台

讓友善同志成為生活日常

2016 年 11 月，婚姻平權大平台誕生。

由台灣同志諮詢熱線協會、台灣同志家庭權益促進會、婦女新知基金會、台灣同志人權法案遊說聯盟、GagaOOLala 同志影音平台協力組成、共同決策，以推動婚姻平權法案為目標，同時也散播愛的故事。

2020 年，婚姻平權大平台轉身成為「彩虹平權大平台」，持續創造「異同共生」的歷史。

同志可以結婚了，但平權之愛仍有更多實踐的空間，為了讓「家」能以更自由的方式長大，為了讓同性戀不再是一種有差別的愛，為了「讓友善同志成為生活日常」，我們致力於透過政治參與、社會教育、國際合作等行動與工作項目，消除因性／別產生的各種不平等，讓友善同志成為生活的日常，邁向多元共好的台灣。

2016 ——與立委尤美女辦公室開始討論並共同提出民法修正草案。

↘ 婚姻平權大平台的開始

2017 ——5 月 24 日大法官釋憲後，持續遊說立法院並在全台舉辦民間講座與展覽活動。

2018 ——面對反同團體積極動員與同志相關公投案，提出「兩好三壞」行動因應，動員一萬名志工、募款千萬，為溝通年齡層較大的中間選民，於報章雜誌公車刊登廣告，同時全台部署培訓對話志工進行民間溝通行動。

2019 ——公投結束後，持續進行同婚立法的政治遊說行動，大型集會也不停歇。5 月 24 日，同性婚姻上路。

終於！我們可以「結婚」了！♥

2020 ——更名為「彩虹平權大平台」，為同婚通過以後的其他權益前進，舉辦參政培訓營，培訓更多同志參與政治。

2021 ——持續推動共同收養、人工生殖、跨國同婚法案，因應疫情採取線上舉辦同婚兩週年活動，並舉辦給大學生的議題倡議營隊。

★ 還有很多目標等著我們完成！

屬於「我們一起」的有意義的數字

➤ 喝過的咖啡杯數超過 15,000 杯。

15,000

➤ 開過 702 場會議。

702

➤ 最常問彼此的一句話:「你午餐要吃什麼?」(下午兩點問……)

➤ 曾製作過 4,809 張彩虹旗,約 1,800,000 份傳單。

4,809　1,800,000

➤ 曾設計過衣服、貼紙、徽章、野餐墊、旗子、枕頭套、杯袋、手鍊、耳環、手帳、明信片、
口罩套、口罩、襪子、背心、毛巾、吊飾、一卡通、啤酒、紅包袋、感謝卡等彩虹周邊。

➤ 夥伴之間常常說的 3 個口頭禪:「OMG 錯誤發言!」「傻爆眼!」「你好好講話!」

➤ 舉辦過 8 場超大型街頭集會活動,與大家一起在立院旁 5 次等待結果。

8　　　　　5

➤ 在凱道前 3 次搖旗吶喊,聚集過 559,000 為自己所相信的價值而站出來的人。

3　　559,000

➤ 每場活動幾乎都有工作夥伴中暑……

➤ 曾在集會看到多種多樣的動物們:大量的狗、鳥、蛇、蜥蜴、貓、烏龜……

➤ 在大型動員最常聽到的話:「怎麼可以叫同志這麼早起!?」

➤ 最早的上班時間:凌晨 12 點活動進場。

12

➤ 最晚的下班時間:活動結束後的凌晨 3 點。

3

➤ 曾發出 96 篇新聞稿與聲明稿。

96

➤ 開過 43 場記者會。

43

➤ 平均每個月 1 場以上的記者會。

1

發出 2 ～ 3 篇新聞稿或聲明稿,提出訴求,向社會發聲。

2-3

➤ 有過 2,325 位參與組織事務的志工夥伴,建立起強壯的線下社群。

2,325

➤ 在 2018 年公投那一年,也在網路上募集了 12,657 位百萬幸福尖兵,串連起有力的線上社群。

12,657

➤ 曾拜會過 65 位立法委員,說服他們投下友善同志的那一票。

65

➤ 也曾拜訪、去電過 105 位議員服務處。

105

➤ 亦曾去電 55 位企業家,尋求贊助和支持。

55

➤ 舉辦了 7 場同志生命故事展,在台北、桃園、台南、高雄,甚至飛到紐約,讓真實的生命故事走入更多人心中。

7

➤ 邀請 908 間公司成為同志友善公司,包含大型企業、書店、咖啡店、婚禮產業……創造更平等有愛的社會環境。

908

➤ 舉辦了 677 場講座、說明會、合作講座、論壇、演講,讓同志社群不斷更新一直在變動的平權運動下一步。

677

➤ 舉辦了 30 場培訓工作坊,除了在執行面上,分享更多的實戰指南,也希望招攬更多有志之士,加入這場漫長的運動。

30

➤ 與 18 個國家進行超過百場國際交流,與美國、英國、日本、紐西蘭、香港、韓國、比利時、加拿大、中國、澳洲、泰國、柬埔寨、菲律賓、越南、捷克、波蘭、黎巴嫩、南非等進行國際交流,希望讓台灣婚權現狀躍上國際。

18

彩虹大平台
歷年設計文宣

為什麼
不同意票
絕不能輸！

表決不能輸

婚權
釋憲
大哉問

萌萌的盲點
大平台來突破

同志也可以
結婚之後

民法不修
歧視不休

七四八
白話文運動

協商不能退

全台
車站

公投怎麼投？
苦不能苦孩子
懶不能懶投票

11月24日
返鄉投票

同志友善
職場指南

Workplace
Equality
Guidebook

未來還沒來
我們一起
前進！

一起 走
我們不會孤單

2020 性平政治怎麼看？

我是 _____ 我支持
婚姻平權修民法
2017 有愛一同

結合 ≠ 結婚
不要一國兩制

即 刻 修 法

婚姻平權
大平台

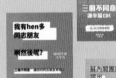

我有hen多
同志朋友

啊然後呢？

蘇內閣團隊
提出
同婚專法草案啦

支持修民法
讓人人都能以愛成家
2017 有愛一同

彩虹政治零距離

是婚姻，才合憲

平等對待 其餘免談！

婚姻平權
大平台

哇！酸甜苦辣的
故事整理魔法

發問，我的群組的大家也很躁動（我昨晚
沒睡，剛剛睡一下醒來，群組就又爆了）
但我覺得愛家還沒有到違法的範圍，可是
志工們在看到愛家就很激動
我可以給什麼樣的建議 😡😡😡

過程

從 2016 年到 2019 年

三年多來

因為有「你」一起走過有淚水、有歡笑、有很多很多愛的過程

我們才有機會一起看見雨過天青的彩虹

雖然公投票數差很多
但是在我們心裡你們是很棒的
未來有機會還是會繼續支持你們

好

我也很擔心○○
台南的志工，昨天
車站發生衝突被指
著罵
之前他自殺過至少
兩次
剛剛發文有點不對
勁，我也在聯絡他

相信我，我們很多異性戀都有
努力跟爸媽談出櫃談教育
無奈的是他們的世代真的很難
接受也有很多社會風氣道德觀
念的影響
不是我們誰不好，每個人都應
該被愛
只是他們還不懂得去愛 😣😣

加油 🐨🐨

也謝謝你們的努力

不是我們的努力，是你們的勇敢！！大家一起加油

謝謝 🐨

* Please turn to page 212 for English version

在愛之前，大家都是平等的。
我是蔡英文，我支持婚姻平權。
讓每一個人都可以自由去愛，追求幸福。
—— 2016.10.31 蔡英文

承繼 2006 年蕭美琴立委提案同性婚姻法、2014 年鄭麗君委員與尤美女委員等人共同提案民法修正案未果後，2016 年，尤美女立委與婚姻平權大平台共同提出婚姻平權的民法修正草案。同年 12 月 3 日，反同方在凱道大集結，假新聞與造謠也激起同志社群的情緒，大平台為鼓舞士氣緊急動員，要讓社會知道，站在街頭上、同志也不會輸——12 月 10 日在世界人權日這一天舉辦「讓生命不再逝去，為婚姻平權站出來」音樂會，召集 25 萬人上凱道，展現了台灣公民的力量。

但在這之前，同志運動已經醞釀 30 年了。

2012 年，時任民進黨黨主席的蔡英文，對台灣伴侶權益推動聯盟所提出的婚姻平權與多元成家法案表態支持，但接下來四年期間，台灣的同志運動路程也不斷犯險前進——2013 年國際間雖有法國國會通過同志婚姻與收養的《344 法案》，但在台灣媒體則看到報導民眾對《認識同志》手冊中性平教育的恐慌，「性平教育進校園」受到阻礙；2014 年尤美女立委與鄭麗君立委皆提案同婚法案並完成一讀，不過當年許多立委迴避拒審，因此未果；2015 年，高雄市、台北市及台中市先開辦同性伴侶註記，讓註記伴侶可簽署手術同意書，但法還沒修，能不能簽仍要視醫療院所的友善與否而定；2015 年，曾於 1986 年到台北地方法院公證處請求與男性公證結婚的祁家威，再度正式向大法官遞交同性婚姻釋憲聲請；同時，因有三對女同志伴侶向台北市戶政事務所申請結婚被拒，台北市政府也因此提起釋憲申請。

2016 年 10 月 16 日，與伴侶同住且相愛 35 年的畢安生教授在愛人曾敬超離世後選擇結束生命，同性伴侶權益無法受到法律保障的事實再度引起社會關注。

同月的同志大遊行，八萬人走上街道。11 月，立法院一讀通過婚姻平權民法修正案，這時候，反同聲浪同時高漲，以「護家」為名的各式團體以「守護家庭」為情感號召，大肆散播恐同訊息。當時婚姻平權公聽會上，留下了許多傷害同志的言論，那是一個謝啟大（前立委）會說：「同志是蟑螂會有連鎖反應」的時代，就連當時世新大學法學院院長吳煜宗也說出同志如「納粹的人體實驗」等偏誤。

我們在荒蠻中挺身前進。那兩個月，不時有大型動員，召集令從臉書活動頁廣傳，只要收到消息，許多人相繼請假前往。12 月 10 日，婚姻平權大平台在凱道上舉辦「讓生命不再逝去，為婚姻平權站出來」音樂會，25 萬人站出來，展現出民意，超過 30 組藝人主動投入無償演出支持。那晚，葉永鋕、林青慧、石濟雅、畢安生，這些因為性別氣質與性向受到傷害的名字，雷射投影於總統府的大面紅磚，以愛之名。人們仰望著那些名字，因為生命的重量流下了眼淚。

那一年，因為群聚的力量，同志們不會再因為「蟑螂連鎖效應」說而喪志，我們也會記得張懸（焦安溥）在公聽會上引美國聯邦大法官所說：「法律難以改變人們的偏見，但法律不可以為偏見服務。」也會記得已經組成同志家庭的杰德影音執行長林志杰所說：「我們要的很簡單，希望在法律保障下，與伴侶和孩子共同生活。」

\# 讓生命不再逝去
\# 為婚姻平權站出來

2016 年 11 月 17 日，立法院司法及法制委員會首次審議民法修正案，反方登四大報動員，一早聚集抗議，辱罵爬牆威脅樣樣來，最後審議不成還加開兩場公聽會。同志運動者們那晚都哭了，決定我們未來會守在街頭不退。 11 月 28 日，第二次民法修正案的公聽會，害怕反同方再次集結干擾，我們召集民眾一早不到九點就在立院外守候，舉辦「相挺為平權，全民撐同志」緊急街頭動員。

Supporters attend an emergency demonstration to show support for the 2016 bill to amend the civil code.

Demonstrators protest against the idea of separate but equal legislation. Their signs read, "I want true equal rights, not separate legislation."

2016 年 12 月 10 日，反同方傳遞出的大量惡意，讓許多年輕同志生命不堪負荷。為了讓政府和社會看見支持同志的力量，在短短三週內我們籌辦了「讓生命不再逝去：為婚姻平權站出來」音樂會，無數名人現身 / 聲支持，超過 25 萬人從台灣各地來到凱道前聲援。

More than 250,000 people attend the largest rally in support of marriage equality in Taiwanese history.

照片提供：沃草

「讓生命不再逝去，為婚姻平權站出來」音樂會現場

Activists project "Fighting For Equality" on the building of the Presidential Office.

2016 年 12 月 26 日，在立法院前舉行了「爭取婚姻平權，用愛守護立院」集會。

Marriage equality supporters gather outside the Legislative Yuan while policymakers deliberate the 2016 marriage equality bill.

為了守護法案的討論程序，我們舉辦了集會。同時，
反同團體也在中山南路集會，為避免兩方衝突，不只
警方加強戒備，強壯的平權夥伴們，還自發性組成了
「平權保衛隊」，站在兩邊的交叉口保護著大家。

2016 年 12 月 26 日這一天，台灣有史以來第一次婚姻平權法案進到委員會入實質審查，跨黨派的支持委員在一週的時間裡，不眠不休、放下歧見，達成難得的共識版本。

The crowd celebrates the first time a marriage equality bill gained the support of multiple political parties.

集會現場，許多人拿著自製標語，傳遞著平權貼紙。

Many marriage equality supporters hold signs urging legislators to revise the civil code.

* Please turn to page 213 for English version

這一年，人們遇到同志，便會說：「恭喜台灣」。但對從事運動的人們來說，婚姻平權尚未看到終點。

5 月 24 日，大法官第 748 號解釋文出爐，宣告同志應受「婚姻自由之平等保障」，不只讓這場歷經三十多年的性別運動，為其他社會運動樹立成功典範，台灣成為亞洲 LGBT 的燈塔，幾年間亞洲區的同志運動也相繼抬頭，日本許多同志伴侶相繼對現行法律排除同婚提起司法訴訟，韓國的同志遊行更盛。

所有支持或參與過運動的人們，背負著傷口走在前方，是為了讓更多人跟上腳步。

釋憲之前，運動者對社會進行許多扎實的部署——婚姻平權大平台專注於與中高年齡層的長輩認識同志，希望敉平社會分歧。2 月，大平台中的四個團體決定接受總統府邀請，與總統進行面對面的對話，之後隨即參考美國聯邦最高法院 Obergefell 案審理過程，向大法官提出「法庭之友意見書」，內含不同專業意見：「『同志生命故事，未完成的權利清單』一人一故事，寫給大法官」完成以精神醫學、心理、法律、社工、教育、政治、性別研究、公衛等專家學者主筆撰寫的同志生命錄。釋憲之後，社會教育的工作也隨即展開——線上線下並行的平權傳播，線上不斷宣導釐清萌萌散布的不實資訊因應釋憲。

5 月 24 日當天，大平台以「『點亮台灣，亞洲燈塔』婚姻平權再戰立院」進行再一次大型動員，同步釋憲動態，那一天，我們帶著緊張的心情前往，釋憲是否通過為未知數，但每個人仍然備齊彩虹旗，現場一如既往地有人發送文宣、有人以花枝招展的服飾為運動祈福，那種一起並肩的心情，與同志大遊行的歡樂不同，彼此間形成一種義無反顧的前進，相視後確認過眼神，給出一個堅定的加油。

傍晚時分，飄起了雨，但人群卻聚集得更多。在司法院秘書長宣告「有關機關應於本解釋公布之日起兩年內，依本解釋意旨完成相關法律之修正或制定。至於以何種形式達成婚姻自由之平等保護，屬立法形成之範圍」時，這些因為運動而堅強的人，全都像小孩一樣流下了眼淚。

雨後，彩虹也來了，像那天站上台發言的蕭美琴所說的那樣：「每個人都值得被愛，每個人都值得被祝福。我們看到台灣的那道彩虹，出現在台灣的天上，世界的天上，人權的天上。」

此後幾個月，大平台持續追蹤法案限制與民情，同時加強同志知識普及，也調度運動的方向，盡可能往成功、最少人受傷的路邁進。當時國際間很關心台灣的婚權狀態，大平台也受邀飛往聯合國人權倡議場合、各大國際組織，甚至是美國國務院內，分享台灣婚姻平權運動現況與進展，當時是總召的欣潔，持續接受著跨越各時區的多國採訪，並且到各海外城市進行演講，盼讓更多人了解台灣。

因為國際的報導，助長了運動氣勢，各地同志遊行參與更盛。大平台也意識到非同溫層溝通的重要性，策略上深入地方，以台語溝通群眾，藉此影響地方議員。不僅與人溝通，大平台也與神同行，跟隨大甲遶境接駕媽祖，接受媽祖的祝福。即便法案像在泥地裡遲滯不前，但運動者仍在掙扎中抬起腳步，往前方邁進。

\# 點亮台灣，亞洲燈塔
\# 婚姻平權再戰立院

2017 年初，我們獲得會見總統的機會，
邀請許多同志伴侶與家庭一同前往，希望
讓府方感受到，在愛裡我們沒有不一樣，
卻可能因法律而遭受不同待遇。

而在知曉大法官即將釋憲的 2017 上半年，大平台窮盡所有能做的努力，同步募集同志故事撰寫成「法庭之友意見書」，提供給每一位大法官；並且在面對每一次反同方的攻擊，都會透過大大小小的講座與記者會，用真實的生命故事，努力闢謠、努力對話。

LGBT rights activists meeting with the President, sending letters to the Grand Justices, and holding press conferences to push for same-sex marriage legalization.

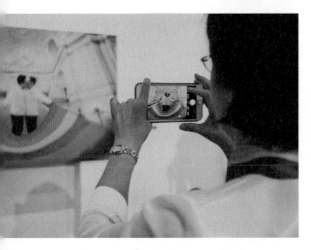

為爭取更多大眾對同志議題的關注，大平台從習俗、信仰、國外經驗、電視、實體展覽，切入群眾日常生活。

我們在過年期間到大稻埕發送平權紅包袋，參與大甲媽祖遶境設壇接駕；邀請加拿大、美國、法國、英國的在台協會代表，與台灣人分享他們國家通過同婚相關法案後，並不會引起社會現況太大波瀾；我們還在全台各地舉辦「愛情故事館：許我們一個未來」展覽，用同志真實的相愛模樣告訴大家，在愛裡，我們都一樣。

Activists raise awareness for the LGBT community through setting up exhibitions, taking part in religious ceremonies, and appearing on TV programs.

2017 年 5 月 24 日大法官釋憲公布的那天，我們和兩萬人再度回到立院旁，希望繼續給政府壓力，加快法案處理的速度。「『點亮台灣，亞洲燈塔』婚姻平權再戰立院」，是為了提醒總統選舉時的承諾，也讓夥伴們知道，我們還不能停止努力，因為真正的平權，還沒到來。

People gather in anticipation of the constitutional interpretation.

當天下午四點，司法院舉行了有史以來第一次中英文記者會，我們就知道，這一刻非同小可。當《釋字第 748 號解釋》出爐時，現場的參與者們都喜極而泣（而我們的電話也被外媒打爆）！

Tears of joy being shed in light of the court ruling in support of same-sex marriage.

這天活動最後的重頭戲是「點亮彩虹台灣」，我們設計了六色透明小卡，邀請群眾一起用手機做一場點亮彩虹的集體行動藝術展演，也提醒執政黨，法案仍須向前推進。這張小卡，陪伴了好多人走到今天。

Flashlights reflect through rainbow filters, lighting the way for marriage equality.

在釋憲通過的這年，我們真的非常期待政府幾個月內就能提出相對應的法案，讓同志權益能邁向下一階段，然而卻遲遲沒有消息……

在當時，時常聽見的「台灣恭喜」，卻是運動推動者有苦難言的一句祝詞，台灣還沒有真的同婚通過，我們還不能掉以輕心，不只是反同方開始宣傳不承認婚姻的伴侶專法，還有不斷造謠誤導大眾的性平教育、課綱修改……在這個時期，大平台持續推動「終止遺憾拒絕等待，婚姻平權就是現在」，所以積極參與各地同志遊行，所以才有了「畢安生紀念晚會」。

Many of the protests and rallies in support of same-sex marriage.

終止遺憾

來不及

2017 年 10 月 16 日，於總統府前舉辦「再也等不到，我們都是畢安生」紀念晚會。

People gather in front of the Presidential Office to commemorate one year since the tragic death of Jacques Picoux.

兩好

第 14 案：「您是否同意，以民法婚姻章保障同性別二人建立婚姻關係？」

第 15 案：「您是否同意，以『性別平等教育法』明定在國民教育各階段內實施性別平等
　　　　　教育，且內容應涵蓋情感教育、性教育、同志教育等課程？」

三壞

第 10 案：「你是否同意民法婚姻規定應限定在一男一女的結合？」

第 11 案：「你是否同意在國民教育階段內（國中及國小），教育部及各級學校不應對學
　　　　　生實施性別平等教育法施行細則所定之同志教育？」

第 12 案：「你是否同意以民法婚姻規定以外之其他形式來保障同性別二人經營永久共同
　　　　　生活的權益？」

* Please turn to page 215 for English version

2018 年，下一代幸福聯盟為首的「愛家」三公投（第 10、11、12 案）成案；苗博雅等人提出的「平權」二公投（第 14、15 案）也成案。

我們逢人就提醒「兩好三壞」。也在那時，許多同志與家人出櫃，和家人討論該怎麼投票，不少分歧，也不少和解。

為了對話，必須建立基礎。大平台在 2018 年初就前往愛爾蘭，也邀請澳洲和美國經歷過公投的同志團體來台，傳授我們如何設定策略與如何應對；同時，努力提供台灣人民許多培訓：在地街頭對話、菜市場與賣場擺攤的行動計畫、團主培訓、認識性平教育、認識同志與同志人權、運用生命經驗融入對話行動，以及，在接近公投時期的情緒與心理課程。

線下婚姻平權小蜜蜂、平權公投小可愛不厭其煩地站在每個捷運站口，與民眾進行第一線的溝通，當然與反方人馬也不時街頭相遇。不斷的記者會、平權講座、策展，更多人因此認識，同志，也是我們的孩子。

公投元年，不同議題同時宣傳，不僅對性別平權運動本身來說困難，對選民而言，也是深具挑戰的一刻。

不斷與下一代幸福聯盟等反同方交鋒的一年裡，假新聞在 Line 裡的流竄讓許多人的家庭群組開始分裂。飛越同溫層的蜂潮行動讓小蜜蜂們去到台北以外的更多地方，在台北以外的講座大大增加。投入更多資源到地方組織，各地方專員組織的志工一同發文宣、做第一線知識溝通，也面臨著大量的不諒解。那年大平台發起「打電話給親人」的記錄活動，讓同志們更勇敢而真實地與生命中重要之人對話。公投以前，「為愛返家，搭上幸福特快車」音樂會，匯聚十萬人，再次凝聚向心力。

11 月 23 日，公投前一天，仍然保有最後一絲希望地傾盡全力，以「回家吧！全台車站接人計畫」在全台火車站，部署拿著舉牌迎接返鄉遊子的志工。

公投結果，我們迎來心碎的一夜。

遭逢公投的失敗，也擔憂這些挫敗在同志們心裡造成傷害，積極舉辦「未來還沒來，我們一起前進」講座。年底的公投結果令人喪志，但令人意外的是，我們居然仍然無法被擊倒。

這場公投的結果，顯示了一年來的草根組織、數位與實體廣告並行、資訊傳播，雖並沒有改變反同方，但仍為我們迎來了三百萬票。在反同方大量資源舖天蓋地襲來之後，大平台的工作重點轉向立法遊說場域，決心不讓同志婚權停在公投的失敗，以盡可能減低同性婚姻與異性婚姻的差距為目標，專法是當時唯一的選擇。

擦乾眼淚，互相扶持，重新整隊，這本是一場資源不對等的戰，漫漫長路，已經走到這裡，還得繼續走下去。

＃ 三個不同意幸福吆
＃ 兩好三壞投出幸福未來
＃ 戀愛返家搭上幸福特快車
＃ 未來還沒來我們一起前進

2018 0126 - 2018 0228

「平等成家，還要等多久？」

兩個媽媽抱著孩子，拍下面色凝重的家庭合照，大平台將照片放上了行政院對面的廣告看板，
邀請民眾與這個同志家庭合影，並向政府提出深切的提問：「平等成家，還要等多久？」

Advocacy groups put up an ad demanding to know, "How much longer before we get equal rights?"

2018 年，是個充滿許多挑戰的一年。面對立院停滯的婚姻平權法案、地方大選中出現在地性別平權議題、反同方以公投挾持大選、鋪天蓋地的假新聞滲透群組與街頭巷尾，但我們不願放棄，持續與社會進行更多溝通與對話。

為了讓公民能與選區立委、議員候選人直接表達意見，我們舉辦「性別公民站出來，爸爸媽媽一起來」地方遊說工作坊；5 月份的國際家庭日透過園遊會，鼓勵同志家庭、年輕爸媽帶著孩子一起來，讓大家看到「家家好家，有愛成家」；並邀請荷、法、澳三國議員來台分享同婚通過歷程，督促政府不應停下腳步。

Marriage equality activists campaigning before the referendum in 2018. At a press conference (left), voters are urged to "vote no for the three anti-equality questions, 10, 11, and 12, and marriage equality will be okay."

在全台灣進入公投白熱化之際，我們串聯全台插旗幟宣傳、去菜市場夜市公園街頭發放文宣、不斷舉辦闢謠記者會，全力投入全國性公投選戰，把握任何可以宣傳的管道、活動……

Activists and organizations campaign all over the island in response to the anti-LGBT agenda pushed by the 2018 referendums.

The circular symbol (left) is the mark stamped by voters on ballots.

投票公投不同意

票公投可不同意不同意

2018 年 11 月 18 日「為愛返家，搭上幸福特快車」兩好三壞音樂會，此次地方大選搭上公投，宣傳等級等同於總統級選戰，所以在選前最後一個黃金周末，我們再度重聚凱道，提醒大家務必返家投票。

The referendum approaching, activists urge young voters to return home in order to vote for equality.

Everyone over 18, we need you to vote on 11/24! Yes on 14 & 16! No on 10, 11, 12!

雨好！ Yes on 14 & 15!

三樓｜No on 10, 11, 12

北北基、桃竹苗、中彰投、嘉南、高屏，
再加上宜花東，我們在這些地方部署草根
組織專員，招募各區域的志工、商家、民
間團體。靠著這群平均年齡25歲以下的組
織專員，讓全台串聯成為可能。

The Marriage Equality Coalition's grassroot
organizers from cities across the country.

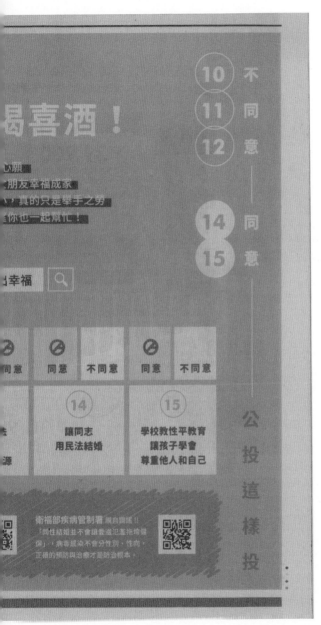

公投這樣投

高齢 93 歲的春桃阿嬤在電視上說，支持 37 歲的孫女小柔與女友結婚，「春桃阿嬤想喝喜酒」的廣告在各大燈箱漾出耀眼笑容，然而⋯⋯

93 year-old Chun Tao, a grandmother who just wants to be able to give a toast at her LGBT granddaughter's wedding.

2018年11月24日，這一晚……

無論如何，我們一起。
在這個巨大宇宙裡，你不是孤單一人。

#開票之夜
#未來雖然還沒來
#但我們 走e前進

2018.11.24 No matter the results, we are in this together. You are not alone.

* Please turn to page 217 for English version

2019 年之初，大平台馬不停蹄地為去年年底的公投結果奔走。

即使整體社會動能看似支持同志族群，但仍不敵反同方資金投注，眼見社群間傳來許多自傷、甚至生命離去的消息，我們努力一面安撫社群情緒、找尋專家提供解方，同時持續進行政治遊說，尋找民法不成的下個解方。

抹掉眼淚，還有路，就得走。

在多方壓力下，行政院蘇貞昌院長於 2 月 21 日提出同婚專法草案《司法院釋字第 748 號解釋施行法》，揭示政府保障同志權益的決心。大平台為爭取國會認同，除了必須不間斷地親自走訪與電訪，亦發起網路動員，邀請網友共同在立委臉書留言，反映最真誠的民意。

快閃舉牌、記者會、社群宣傳、票數計算、信心喊話⋯⋯我們做了能做的，但總是覺得還不夠，與大家一樣，這真是一段期待又怕再度受傷害的日子，時間步步逼近。

5 月 17 日終於到來，下著大雨，人們站在雨裡的目光堅定，發自內心地喊出「表決不能輸」，希望同志們為彼此、為更多生命撐下去。焦急、緊張、悲傷、盼望⋯⋯隨著一條一條法案在螢幕上出現，一個又一個燈號亮起，我們不敢相信這個一直相信著的信念，眼淚奪眶、緊緊相擁，啊，真的過了，真的，可以結婚了。

天氣在最後一刻放晴，就算老套也想說「就跟我們的心情一樣」！這是同志們慶祝的好日子！五萬多人站在立法院前，再多泥濘的路都走過，所以不怕淋濕，共同迎接歷史的瞬間，一起見證立法院三讀通過同婚專法的時刻，多少對新人在這場大雨之前就以愛允諾彼此,他們共同生活多年,欠缺的只是一張紙,啊,真的過了,真的,可以結婚了。

返家後仍然過著炊食相愛、盥洗梳頭、吵鬧又和好的日常,卻是更理直、更氣壯、更溫暖、更柔軟的日常,終於,我們可以說:「給我們的紅包,可以開始準備了!」

5 月 24 日,同婚專法上路的第一天,太陽高掛,是一個結婚的好日子。大平台於台北、高雄舉辦聯合婚禮,同時與台北市政府民政局合辦「幸福起跑線 Wedding Party」,交往 10 年的陳雪與早餐人、甫投入熱烈愛情的厭世姬與簡莉穎,都在這一天終於完成了登記。那一天,超過五百對同志伴侶填滿了彼此的配偶欄,相愛就是這樣一件微小但真實確定的事,同婚終於雨過天青了。

\#協商不能退
\#表決不能輸
\#一個都不能少
\#雨過天青
\#幸福起跑線
\#台灣同婚元年

2019 年，《司法院釋字第 748 號解釋》即將滿兩週年，反同方終於提出他們所說的「專法」：一個沒有「婚姻」二字，只有共同生活卻不能「結婚」的專法……

同志團體努力拜會立委服務處、召開大大小小記者會；呼籲行政院院長守住憲法解釋防線，法案裡一定要有「婚姻」二字；回應特殊專法，提出「婚姻不要一國兩制」，而這一句話在日後，也成為主要訴求、集會手牌標語。於此同時，同志家庭與家人、孩子的權益成為新的攻防戰場，要「結婚」，要「收養」，才是對同志家庭孩子們的最大保障。

Activists hold press conferences and lobby policymakers as the deadline to legalize same-sex marriage approaches.

同年 5 月 14 日、5 月 17 日，到了同婚法案審查
的最後程序，這兩天有超過五萬人來到青島東
路，對著立委，也對我們自己說：「協商不能
退！」 「表決不能輸！」

The final day of deliberation and the day of the
vote. More than 50,000 people gather to witness
the historical moment.

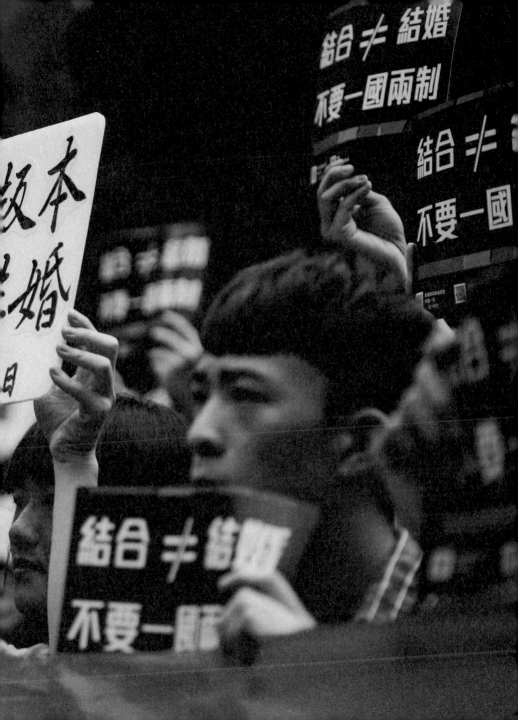

2019 年 5 月 14 日的「協商不能退」青島東集會，立委們在「同性婚姻」、「同性伴侶」還是「同性結合」這之間無法取得共識，就得先進入黨團協商的程序，但對同志來說，「婚姻」二字退無可退，我們只能請大家在三天後的 5 月 17 日再次站上街頭，捍衛最後底線。

Protesters demand the right to marriage, not partnerships, and not civil unions!

這是一個民主多元的社會：）

Anti-LGBT rights groups disrupt a rally in support of same-sex marriage.

Democracy is alive in Taiwan.

同志已經退無可退

2019 年 5 月 16 日，我們
在忠孝西路天橋、立院前
進行了舉牌快閃行動。

Activists stage a flash mob
before the vote to make a
final statement denouncing
any compromise of equal
rights

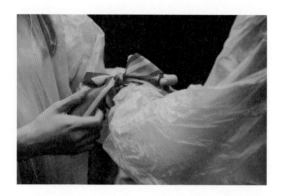

2019 年 5 月 17 日，又一次來到青島東路。這三年半和大家一起在街頭為平權奮戰，終於來到法案表決投票的這天。一早，灰濛濛的天空看起來馬上就會下雨，但不到九點，超過萬人已來到立院旁的青島東路上，「表決不能輸」，我們要讓議場裡投票的委員們知道，大家都在這裡，支持台灣走向更平等的這一步。

More than 10,000 supporters surround the Legislative Yuan at 9 a.m. on voting day.

法案表決前有討論，接著是逐條按表
決器的漫長過程，早上九點立院開始
開會的時候天空越來越暗，逐條表決
的時候雨越下越大，人們舉起一把把
的傘，緊盯著表決的數字，守護的不
是傘下的自己，而是可以跟別人一樣
結婚的未來。

The crowd braves the pouring rain
outside the Legislative Yuan to   wait
for the results of the vote.

法案全文三讀通過的議事槌敲下，在國際反恐同日的這天，台灣成為亞洲第一個通過
同性婚姻的國家。

As the bill is passed, Taiwan becomes the first country in Asia to legalize same-sex marriage.

從大雨轉為晴天，還出現了彩虹，那天的天空，跟著我們的心情一起雨過天青。

As the rain subsides, a rainbow emerges. A true calm after the storm.

早上竟然下雨，大家辛
苦了ＱＱ

風雨生信心！！！大家
一起加油！！

如果淋雨了，還是趕緊擦
乾，不要感冒了，大家今天
辛苦了，一起度過！

20 和 24 條也過了～～
恭喜大家～

分享醜哭照給大家

真的太好了ＱＱ

太哭了！！

😍 5

竟然出現彩虹

這是什麼巴辣劇情

太扯了啦

對不起我沒禮貌

但真的太誇張

131

2019 年 5 月 24 日，同志，終於可以結婚了。那在風中在雨中街頭並肩作戰的日子，終於走過，迎來了豔陽高照的婚禮，還有充滿愛與粉紅泡泡的愛人們相擁著。我們一起見證伴侶們決定攜手承諾的這一天，同時也是台灣讓世界驚豔的這一天。

同志，終於可以結婚了！

May 24, 2019, the first day samo ocx couples can legally get married in Taiwan.

我們邀請了 20 對同性伴侶一起聯合登記結婚，慶祝也熱鬧著，台北市信義戶政事務所貼心的將所有櫃檯燈號換成「524」，也放上可愛的小彩虹旗，共同迎接來登記的同性伴侶。

At the household registration office, the staff have decorated in order to welcome same-sex couples.

At 29th Street, New York

2019 年，台灣的我們在平權運動上邁進了一大步；2019 年也正逢美國石牆事件 50 週年，大平台前往紐約參訪、策展、遊行，在國際間看見台灣如何前進的同時，台灣也開始找尋性別平權的下一個方向。

The Marriage Equality Coalition attends a demonstration for the 50th anniversary of the Stonewall Riots in New York to celebrate "the First in Asia" with the world.

* Please turn to page 218 for English version

2020 年，婚姻平權大平台正式更名為「彩虹平權大平台」，為了持續創造異同共生的歷史，光譜的每一端都該大放異彩。除了政治倡議與遊說、更往社會溝通教育與國際合作札根，那場年底公投讓運動者認知，意識形態的轉變並非一朝一夕，他們已經準備好，用一百萬隻蝴蝶的振翅，吹動社會的風向。

在平權立法面馬不停蹄，大平台不僅召開共同收養法案與各方的會議，也與同家會攜手協助了 15 組代孕男同志爸爸個案，3 次跨國同婚個案協調溝通會議，與進行 33 場行政調整程序會議。2020 年底，共同收養草案獲得了 20 位立委支持，順利一讀通過。

同志要結婚、還得先出櫃，敢不敢請婚假、擺囍宴，都是挑戰，要救平職場的歧視，持續對話分享故事、企業內部培訓都不能少。大平台從 2020 年到 2021 年持續追蹤民情，《社會態度研究調查》顯示無論是從職場、到校園、或是社會，平權都尚待完備。同婚過後，邀請

彩虹公民繼續走上街頭，不是為了說服，而是要了解異溫層，看見台灣的真實。

處在數位溝通的時代，又逢疫情，為了持續做社會溝通，大平台決定在數位平台上以輕鬆的角度推廣同志生命面貌──「我的出櫃時代」、「同志歸同志，政治歸政治？」、「我就玻璃心！職場的部分～」，以親民與真實的對話接觸數位民族。Podcast 「欸姐來跟你說」以前輩角度談失戀、從台灣角度談國際同志大事，從生理、心理到世界的面面俱到，相比拚公投與召集令，是更細水長流的倡議工作。

同運 30 年，運動者們都知道，一路上的耕耘非一蹴可幾，同婚後的細緻溝通工作，需要更多耐心與專注，大平台持續在政府與民間穿梭，為了讓專法、同性戀沒有區別，從倡議升級行政表格系統先著手，修改行政表格中「父母」、「夫妻」之欄位，大至政策、小至系統，都需要監督與修改。而政治的改變，需要更多的同志願意跳進政治擾

動，全台第一場同志參政培訓營發生了，伴著有志之士一步步走，讓同溫層更壯大。

2021 年的 4 月，蔡佩汶與伴侶在保守的情治單位見證下成為一家人，法務部長蔡清祥，三名調查局前後任局長都到場祝賀。5 月時，阿古與信奇的台澳聯姻，在伴侶盟的辯護下，取得了台灣跨國同婚司法訴訟案上的重要勝利。

同時，我們在社群上看見製作人陳鎮川公布與伴侶迎來新生兒的幸福照片，感受到生命的祝福同時，不忘還有許多家庭在等，跨國婚姻、收養法案、人工生殖，是兩年來運動的核心目標。更多的故事，在台灣被看見，縱使因為疫情許多計畫打掉重練，但更不忘眾志成城的意志。

一週年的同婚週年慶已因 2020 年的疫情取消，2021 年大平台決議不論如何，一定要跟曾一起走來的大家們共同歡慶。原先預定集會的同婚兩週年活動改為線上舉辦「彩虹來照路，做伙鬥鬧熱」線上群聚，

鼓舞士氣，也同樣在疫情時刻，凝聚台灣人的向心力。同時推出「平權認同卡」，拿出一卡通的同時也是遞出友善，讓愛落實成日常。

疫情在跑，平權不能等，持續研議法案修正與不間斷的政治倡議，讓同性婚姻可以與異性戀婚姻一樣，不受到國籍的限制，相愛的彩虹能在台灣這片土地上遍地開花；改變同婚專法中同志僅能收養配偶的「親生子女」的條件，讓婚後與配偶共同收養的平等落實，家也沒有高低之分；為了讓那些遠渡跨海到美國、加拿大等地使用人工生殖技術生下孩子的同志家庭，可以在自己的國家進行人工生殖手術，推動人工生殖法等相關法規修正。

大平台在意的是真實的人們，共融共存不是口號，而是實踐。持續發光，讓同志社群的權利得到更完整的照護，曾經一起站上街頭的人，回到生活裡落實相愛。

此刻，未來，彩虹旗還在飄揚。

在同婚法案通過的這條路上，

努力推動法案進程的立委、默默改變社會的政治幕僚、

接納多元的同志牧師、溫柔理解的櫃父母解惑者、

用力表態支持的公眾人物、認真努力的第一線志工，

有許多人，與我們一起並肩而行。

尤美女 × 許毓仁

尤美女，時為民進黨不分區立委、現為律師
許毓仁，時為國民黨不分區立委、現為台灣玉山科技協會秘書長

* Please turn to page 220 for English version of Mei-Nu Yu & Yu-Jen Hsu

在尤美女和許毓仁兩位還擔任立委時，當年他們的辦公室恰好在同一層，他們時不時在電梯前碰面，並重複以下對話：

「我會問他：『啊你們國民黨現在怎麼樣？（笑）』。」
「我就會說『我不知道』，反問她民進黨怎麼樣，她就會說她『也不知道』。」

這段對話反映的，或許是兩位在推動同婚法案時有多邊緣。2019年 5 月，《司法院釋字第 748 號解釋施行法》投票日前，民進黨所有協商都將尤美女排除在外，「他們理由是說，反正我要講什麼他們都知道了，可能怕我去跟對方起衝突吧。」好長一段時間，時不時會有選區立委抓著她說，「尤美女我會被你害死」。

許毓仁的狀況當然也沒好到哪去，身為政壇菜鳥，照三餐被黨內大老施壓「不要出聲、不要投票、不要吵」，表決前一天，他也接到了關切電話：「我被勸說不要發言，但投票前還是上台講了。下來之後坐我旁邊的委員就說：『我不是叫你不要上去講嗎？』之後我每按一個贊成，他就一把火燒起來。」他回憶此事，有點調皮地說，想知道是哪一位委員，大家就自己上網查查看吧。

為人權，逆風三十年

為了支持同婚，兩人將被討厭的勇氣補好補滿。對尤美女而言，婦運背景絕對是她能支撐下去的原因，「參加婦運之後，開始有自信，我不再在乎別人的眼光。我所在乎的是自己的所作所為到底是對是錯，還要為自己負責。」1980 年代加入婦女新知基金會，攤開戰績，洋洋灑灑，性別工作平等、子女姓氏修法都有她在背後大力推動。

進入立院後更是火力全開，家事事件法、夫妻財產制、通姦除罪化，越艱難越要推，雖千萬人吾往矣。2012 年，尤美女第一次提出同婚民法修正案，到 2019 年同婚以專法形式通過，走了 7 年，路程磕磕碰碰，令人沮喪的事不少，但她從未想過放棄。

「我從事婦運 30 年，跟婦女權益有關的法案，幾乎每一個都要將近 10 年的時間，而且都是在一個事件爆發，不是有人去世就是有人受傷的情況下才能夠通過。」

她以民法親屬編子女姓氏條文修正案為例，推動數年，才在 2007 年修法，規定父母雙方得以書面約定讓子女從父姓或母姓；2010 年又再次修正，讓成年人得以自主改姓。

「光是想改個姓氏，我們當年就被罵得狗血淋頭，鋪天蓋地的報導，人類學者、姓名學者、記者都寫專欄來罵我們。可是過了兩年多，2010 年我們再修改到成年者可以自己去改姓，社會一點聲音都沒有。」前面的第一關是最恐怖的，尤美女熟悉這種搖動巨大結構會造成的反彈，因而有堅定的膽量，只要方向是對的，逆風也要走下去。

我所在乎的是自己的所作所為是對是錯，還要為自己負責。

沒有包袱，就是優勢

許毓仁身為一個闖入保守政黨的政治素人，也沒有任何社運背景，為何要為同婚發聲？許毓仁說起當年擔任行政院青年顧問，或許就是因此被前行政院長毛治國賞識，將他放入不分區立委名單，而他之所以答應，是以為自己只會是個陪榜仔。沒想到名單一出，第五順位，當下直接「賀，當選」。

眾人看許毓仁這一步棋，霧裡看花，連尤美女都嚇一大跳，「在他當立委前我們就認識，就我對他的了解，他應該是被民進黨提名，怎麼會去國民黨？我是非常錯愕的（笑）。」難道自己識人不明？她陷入自我懷疑。

許毓仁笑說，民進黨沒來找他啊，「反正我本來也沒有什麼政黨色彩，覺得這樣保守的政黨，如果有不一樣的聲音，或許可以被攪動。如果我在任的時候，可以讓雙方在一些議題裡有個橋樑也不錯，這是為什麼我願意進去做的原因。」來自思想進步的新創圈，他也明白自己會遇到質疑：「但我想用行動表示，等人家回頭來看看我做了什麼。」

反正從政是意外，他自認沒什麼好失去的，便以 4 年為目標，試著讓國家更接近他心中理想的樣子。

2016 年選上立委，恰好碰上婚姻平權的浪潮，出身於擁抱多元的新創圈，他對同志的認同是天然的。一次出差經驗，更讓他理解同志的困境，「那次一位同事在飛機上和我說她是同志，但她不敢跟家人講，心裡面很多掙扎，還要面對不一樣的眼光，其實那一次對我影響很大。當立委之後，覺得如果我們這少數的一百多人，有權力去改變歷史的話，那我應該去推動。」他先在國是論壇投下震撼彈，說希望「台灣成為亞洲第一個同婚合法化的國家」，也進一步在國民黨內推起同婚修法。

當時，尤美女是司法及法制委員會召委，掌握了排案的權力，但她身為執政黨立委，也須顧全大局，有時做起事來手腳不如許毓仁自由。「當時我跟尤委員有個默契，分屬在野黨、執政黨，我們可以互相扮演好自己的角色。」作為國民黨裡的孤鳥，許毓仁將自己設定為長程火砲，「我直接提民法、提到最進步的版本，負責進攻。」反對黨的委員怎麼比執政黨更進步？他希望這種作法能給執政黨帶來推進的壓力。

各司其職，衝破阻力

當時黨內大老們並不把許毓仁當一回事，「我拿草案給黨內的委員簽，他們都簽了，可能覺得小孩子不懂事，反正這案子也排不進去。結果我運氣很好，有十幾個委員簽了，還包含王金平這些資深委員，他們可能也不知道自己簽了什麼（笑）。」

2016 年底，尤美女、許毓仁、時代力量黨團分別提出民法修正草案版本，其中許毓仁的版本竟是在這樣誤打誤撞下產生的。

兩人回憶起 2016 年 11 月 17 日法案審查的景況。當天，尤美女坐在主席台，國民黨要求先開 30 場公聽會才能繼續審理法案，甚至衝上主席台爆發肢體衝突。

「我趕快聯絡同志團體討論，大家就堅決說一場都不能開，因為每次開公聽會他們就像錄音機一樣一直重複，可是國民黨也不肯退，兩邊就一直拉鋸。」僵持到下午四點多，總務處長緊張地請尤美女趕快散會，外頭抗議群眾已經要衝進來了。

「他說，委員妳再不散會會有生命危險。」當時，雙方已協調到將公聽會由 30 場改成兩場，但國民黨仍不願簽字，直到眼看緊急散會在即，他們才在最後一刻簽了下去。「一簽完，台下馬上就有一個假記者衝上來，被法警制止，外面也有很多叫囂的群眾，真的還滿緊張的。」她說，也不曉得為什麼國民黨肯簽字，但法案能通過，靠的真的就是這些「突然通了」的時間點。

「後來得知，同志團體透過各種管道，去找國民黨的關鍵支持者打電話給大老們，遊說他們稍微讓一下。也很感謝他們。」

而當天，對立院小白兔許毓仁而言絕對是震撼教育，過去只能在電視上看見的立委打架，竟在眼前真實上演，「那天真的非常非常緊張，一開始就衝突了，那時候應該是鄭天財吧，衝去把麥克風扯掉。」眼見黨內同志身先士卒，身為黨的一員的標準動作為何？「我很尷尬，到底要不要上去，整場我就是非常尷尬……」可惜，沒有一本專出給新手立委的潛規則教科書。表決是否贊成召開公聽會時，許毓仁沒有舉手，看見黨內同志的眼光，馬上體悟：「那次之後，我就很清楚明白，這條路上會遭遇到非常大的困難跟阻力。」

11 月 17 日排案審查，因部分立委及民眾強烈反對引發肢體衝突，雙方協議先由許淑華、尤美女二位召委於 11 月 24 日及 28 日分別召開一場公聽會後，再次審查。12 月 26 日，三個提案版本順利融合成修正《民法》和另立專法的兩個版本，正式送出委員會。無論一開始有多少歧見，最終和平達到現階段共識，尤美女認為，這是成熟民主的證明。

公投大敗，彼此拍拍再走下去

2017 年 5 月 24 日，大法官以《釋字第 748 號解釋》釋憲，認為民法未使相同性別二人合法結婚，違背憲法精神；並要求兩年內修法，否則兩年後，同志將可直接以民法登記結婚。解釋文一出，將婚權運動推到最高峰，反同方更是心急如焚，眼見 2018 年公投綁大選是兩年內唯一發聲的大好機會，便開始全面集結。挺同方也不甘示弱跟隨提案，卻迎來意料之外的全面挫敗。

自認已經在過退休生活的尤美女，招牌造型不變，桃紅正裝外套，髮絲間有大紅色挑染。憶起公投結果，她歷歷在目：

「公投之後整個 down 下來，非常挫敗。對很多同志而言，有些人會覺得是不是要放棄？可是我個人覺得，都已經走到這個地步來，民進黨行政、立法又全面執政。我們的核心價值是自由、民主、法治、人權，沒道理因為公投挫敗而結束。」

本業為律師，她在挺同方一片士氣低迷中，理性釐清局面：我們還沒有輸。

「2018 年的挫敗，其實只是說沒有辦法再修民法，只能用專法。我比較焦慮的是，到底是什麼樣的專法？雖然大法官已經講得很清楚，要保障同志婚姻自由平等的權利，但有沒有可能再訂出一個違憲的法律？」一旁的許毓仁則說，當時同婚被大選挾持，淪為各候選人動員跟操作的議題，非常可惜。

「所以在公投挫敗之後，整個社會氛圍是強烈的反對狀態。我受到滿大的壓力，因為那時候國民黨算是 2018 年縣市長選舉大勝，黨內的保守勢力也抬頭。」看，我們就是因為反同，才能贏得選舉，這股氣勢還想延續到 2020 總統大選，你許毓仁何苦擋路？

尤美女也在此時遭遇到黨團嚴重的孤立，總召柯建銘甚至在媒體面前說：「拜託尤美女妳放了民進黨！」她苦思良久，想不到如何回應，隔天睡醒才靈光一閃，「我請助理去查，發現公投過後同志自殺、受霸凌的案件有增加趨勢，我就以這個數據回應媒體，把話題轉開。」如此回應，不但化解了差點發展成黨內衝突的話題，也給了許多挺同夥伴勇氣：

「我是非常非常感動，有很多不認識的同志朋友，甚至異性戀朋友勇於表達，會打電話甚至寄卡片來，不斷地安慰我或是表示感謝，真的很可愛。我們這個年紀，可能都會藏在心裡，可是現在年輕人真的不一樣，我感受滿深刻的。我們辦公室就有一面牆，全是各方的來函。」

而許毓仁的辦公室也有這樣一面牆。三年了，公投票數公布那晚的低迷氣氛仍令人難忘，只是哭過之後，我們用意志及行動證明了，只要彼此牽著手不放，最終一定能穿越那些不理解、甚至惡意的目光。

雨過天青，彩虹乍現

時間來到 2019 年 5 月 17 日，《司法院釋字第 748 號解釋施行法》表決前一晚，行政院長蘇貞昌與所有民進黨立委商討政策方向時，發表了一席話。尤美女說，那很關鍵。

「蘇院長非常感性，講了民進黨是怎麼過來的。當年大家是提著頭顱，而現在只是幾張選票而已，竟然這麼退卻？以後有一天，你的孫子問你：『當年有沒有投贊成票？』你該怎麼講？這是時代的潮流，我們應該站在對的地方。」

蘇貞昌接著也在臉書發文，呼籲民進黨要為同婚議題歸隊。同一時間，許毓仁有點憂心，「我擔心這件事又要回到政治對決。當下就有人在群組說，民進黨歸隊了，那我們國民黨也要歸隊，團進團出，沒有灰色地帶。」

「以後有一天，你的孫子問你：『當年有沒有投贊成票？』你該怎麼講？」

因此，投票當日早上的黨團大會，他希望將大家的心拉回價值面，「我說，民進黨好像把這個議題升高成政黨對決，但是我們不要這樣做，希望還是讓我們支持的價值被凸顯。」不同黨派，不同觀點與作法，最終寫下了臺灣人權歷史上重要的一頁。

兩人都懷抱著擔心票數不夠的焦慮踏入立院，直到看見一個個綠燈亮起，關鍵的第四條、第七條都奇蹟似地過關。尤美女激動不已，同黨立委何志偉興奮地拿著手機衝過來，「尤委員、尤委員，留言都湧進來了，大家喊妳是媽祖婆、觀世音菩薩」；許毓仁腦中則出現自己這四年短暫政治生涯的跑馬燈，原來這就是當立委的感覺，原來自己完成了一件了不起的事情。

立院外大雨停歇，彩虹乍現，眾人歡呼擁抱。尤美女與許毓仁兩位委員，站在自己認為是對的信念裡，替許許多人帶來了難以量測的幸福。

「什麼是 ？」Q & A

●什麼是正常？

許：正常或不正常，是一個過度簡化、區分我們所存在的這個世界的方式。一去區分正常，就會有不正常，所以我不會這樣想。

尤：正常通常是多數人或是執政者、掌權者去界定的。主流就正常，非主流就不正常。我們在講性別主流化就是讓這些被邊緣化的到核心來，接著再繼續把更邊緣的人主流化。

●什麼是愛？

許：愛就是用同理心去感受身邊的人。你能不能愛他人跟愛你自己是一樣的？

尤：愛最重要的其實是無條件的付出。很多人都說他必須怎樣我才會愛他，他如果不是怎樣就不愛他，這樣還叫作愛嗎？

李懷仁

行政院某個角落裡，一位男子正在筆記本上塗塗改改。「誰是穩的，誰是不穩的，誰又是一定抓不過來的？」他心情忐忑，表決只剩下兩週，他還能動用哪一層關係固票？黨內大老們答應要打的電話都打了嗎？

「我們 5 月開始，每天都估一遍票數，因為每天都有變化。不知道你們有沒有看過影集《白宮風雲》？其實就很像那個場景。」資深政治幕僚李懷仁說。

關鍵第 4 條

在 2019 年 5 月 17 日表決前，李懷仁沒有一刻是放鬆的。直到最後他都擔心票數不足，甚至害怕有人跑票引起連鎖效應，最終兵敗如山倒。「其實我們透過黨內各個意見領袖，不斷地溝通，到了最後兩三天，知道說票不一定會開得漂亮，但應該有機會過關。」只是，單純過關怎麼夠？對台灣社會而言這麼重要的法案，一定要用絕對多數通過才能一絕後患。

「如果用簡單多數過，很可能改天又被簡單多數推翻，所以我們每天都會讓總統、院長等高層長官知道預估票數，目標就是要催出過半的選票。」馬不停蹄固票，未達目的前，關切的電話將陰魂不散。「政治上的複式動員，以民間的說法可能是情緒勒索（笑），同一個委員會接到和他關係不錯的委員的電話、院長的電話、某部長的電話，請他務必要出來投票。」針對同婚議題，各方已經以理探討、辯論了好長一段時間，最後一刻，要動之以情。

複式動員、蘇院長溫情喊話，以結果來看，他們成功了，而且效果超乎預期。「第 1 條的時候很緊張，票開出來變很興奮，怎麼會七十幾票那麼多？接著最關鍵的第 4 條投出來過半，當下就聽到外面群眾的歡呼聲，我的 LINE 群組一直跳出『哇』，就確定穩了。」他說，接下來所有條文的票數他都不記得了，上緊的發條鬆開了。

「成立第二條關係應以書面為之，有二人以上證人之簽名，並應由雙方當事人，依司法院釋字第 748 號解釋之意旨及本法，向戶政機關辦理結婚登記。」──《司法院釋字第 748 號解釋施行法》第 4 條

結婚，這兩個字對某些人來說實在太敏感，提及這兩個字的第 4 條、第 7 條到底會不會過？很讓支持者擔心。李懷仁印象深刻，當時法案得以保留「結婚」的說法，靠的是行政院長蘇貞昌的堅持，「在法案要出行政院前，最後有幾個版本在定案，各方還有一點角力，主要就是在要不要有『婚姻』的說法。」他回憶，針對歧見，蘇院長是這麼說的：

「我從當美麗島律師到現在，一輩子在幫大家爭公平的權利。為什麼他們要結婚這兩個字，我們不能給？」

我從當美麗島律師到現在，一輩子在幫大家爭公平的權利。為什麼他們要結婚這兩個字，我們不能給？

法案的版本就此定了調。「那段話讓我滿感動的，那不是在對外演說時慷慨激昂的表演，只是私底下在跟我們幾個幕僚討論時的真情流露，就是他信奉的價值。你說我們會不會算選票？會，可是有些東西不是這樣算的。」他說起 1979 年的美麗島大審判，「當時幫忙辯

護的，第一波就被抓走，但蘇院長第二波還願意上去。」他說，如果蘇貞昌每件事都要算計，當初就不會站上去了。

民進黨幕僚眼中的十年同婚路

擔任蘇貞昌的政治幕僚十多年，他第一次在政治上處理到同志議題，是在 2010 年蘇貞昌的台北市長選戰中。當時，團隊考量台北是對同志相對開放的城市，也許可以試著推動看看，友好同志配音員賈培德便建議蘇貞昌參與當年的同志大遊行。

「那時候公開支持同志的政治人物其實不多，蘇院長是其一。不過後來同志大遊行並不歡迎他，可能因為對他的立場比較不了解，覺得他是要去收割。」10 年前吃了同運閉門羹的他們，從沒想過不到 10 年後，台灣竟會成為亞洲第一個同婚合法化的國家，「以政治幕僚的角度來看，是知道台灣應該要開始準備類似的立法，比方說先在不動到法律的情況下，想出一些權宜措施，像後來各縣市有做的伴侶註記，其實圈內都會有這樣的討論。但真的沒設想到 2019 年就會成功。」

他爬梳民進黨與社運團體的關係，2000 年到 2008 年是民進黨與社會運動分手的過程，2000 年第一次政黨輪替，陳水扁的當選與社運團體脫不了關係，然而這份信任卻在往後的八年中逐漸磨損。「08 年、10 年那時，民進黨失去社運團體的支持，又剛在野，狀況是很弱勢的。」在他眼中，蘇、蔡兩人對於同志的支持，自始至終沒有變過，只是在不同時空背景、政治環境下，會造就大家對他們的不同觀感。

「比方說 2016 年，小英總統在選前表達支持同婚，當選後卻被同志團體罵不夠認真，覺得都執政了怎麼推這麼慢？但事實其實是 16 年到 17 年陷入了民法、專法的大戰，只要是專法派就被貼上歧視的標籤，那時大家還不知道專法是社會比較能接受的版本。」心之所向與政治判斷之間，總是有段差距，「我承認我是民法派，但我深深知道，當時在政治上的處理恐怕只能走到專法。」這段差距，就是政治人物與民眾容易產生摩擦的地方。幸好，台灣社會最終達成了階段性的共識。

「也許你當下不會這樣覺得，但如果回頭看，走到目前的狀況，其實是集體的智慧。大法官說要保障同婚權利，民意說不要動民法，所以最後走到專法。這是台灣社會從法律到行政到民意的集體產物，所有力量的交集。」

《司法院釋字第 748 號解釋施行法》並不完美，但它已經是台灣社會經過長時間拉扯後，彼此之間得出的最大交集。

同婚之後，太陽依然升起

能產出這樣的結果，法案的命名至關重要。2017 年 5 月，大法官以《司法院釋字第 748 號》宣告民法不讓相同性別之二人合法結婚有違憲法，並給出兩年的修法大限。2019 年 2 月，眼見死線在即，法案一定得送，眾人卻為案名頭痛不已。

「當時討論的，一個是同性伴侶法，一個是同性婚姻法。但送伴侶法，同志團體一定罵翻；送婚姻法，宗教團體一定罵翻。」時任總統府副秘書長、現任（2021 年）考試院秘書長劉建忻，與幾位資深政治幕僚在會議裡想到破頭，「劉副秘在美國讀研究所，靈機一動想到，像美國有很多第幾號施行法，我們何不把大法官釋字當作法案名稱？另外，我們借用台灣的兩公約施行法，把兩個概念融合在一起。」好像解套了！在場眾人按捺喜悅，各自回頭試探自家長官、友好的民間團體。

「那時我就問了欣潔，請她低調詢問同仁意見，後來發現同志團體可以接受而且覺得是不歧視的，我們就比較有信心。當然也問過宗教團體，他們也覺得沒有婚姻這兩個字，可以接受。」

行政院勇敢提出這個名稱中性的法案，成為台灣立法上的全新創舉，「同志團隊也好像注入了強心針，這個政府輸成這樣還願意提一個不是很專法的專法，而是感覺包著專法名義的民法。也希望大家每次讀到這部法，會想起它是大法官釋憲的結果，全台灣最懂法律、最有公信力的一群人做的結論。」政府與社運團體不再脫節，既然目標一致，在步伐及手段上能如何互相配合、調整、牽制、妥協？李懷仁認為，同婚運動為此做了一次良好的示範，可為其他議題借鏡。

法案一定名，政治幕僚們就馬上布線媒體記者、製作相關懶人包，更請蘇院長親自拍片解釋，確保民眾能理解法案的價值與內涵。三讀通過後，他們也沒閒著，把原本只是內政部民政司管理層級的婚姻登記表，送進行政院內一格一格檢查，高規格對待，就是希望這部法案頒布後沒有任何歧視字眼，不出分毫差錯。

「我們希望讓大家看見，法案通過，台灣社會照樣運作。太陽一樣升起，爸爸叫爸爸、媽媽叫媽媽，你的小孩本來要生不會變不生、兒子本來喜歡女生不會變喜歡男生。喜歡男生就是喜歡男生，喜歡女生就是喜歡女生，我們只是把原本該有的權利還給他。」

已離開幕僚圈，南下高雄擔任一卡通董事長的李懷仁，回憶起這段為人權奮鬥的歷程，仍像個熱血青年，雙眼發亮，一股熱情隨時要從胸口衝出來。我問他，不想念嗎？他笑說，心會癢。

「但兩年前三讀完那一天，我回到行政院就跟院長說，我覺得我的政治幕僚生涯已經到頂了，我可以離開了，真的，跟你打完這一仗，我沒有什麼遺憾了。」

無論哪天會不會又在蘇院長跟前看到他的身影，這位政治幕僚為同婚所做的努力，已經深深刻進歷史裡。

「什麼是 ？」Q & A

● 什麼是平等？

每個人的權利都應該是一樣的。我常常跟小孩子講，不能歧視、霸凌別人，因為每個人都是一樣的。

● 什麼是正常？

沒有必要去定義誰是正常，因為正常跟不正常是相對的，當你去定義我們是正常，才會有別人是不正常。

2019.5.16 立院表決前日，蘇貞昌向民進黨立院黨團溫情喊話

明天就是歷史的關鍵時刻了，各位委員有的做一屆，有的做好幾屆。大家在立法院通過的法案幾百、幾千件，但將來可以拿出來談的、拿出來講的，其實不多。將來一定會被問到的，一定有明天同婚這一案。到那時候，整個社會進步到那裡了，你可以拍胸脯、很大聲地說：「你看，當年壓力是多麼大，但我還是頂下來了，我投下關鍵的一票！」當然，你也可能被自己的孩子、孫子問到：「當年那歷史性的時刻、歷史性的一天，你為什麼沒有站出來？」

各位，40 年前美麗島事件、軍法大審的時候，全台灣有近千位律師。但真正敢站出來、只有我們 15 個；33 年前民主進步黨組黨的時候，其實真正簽名的沒有那麼多人。因為那時候會被抓、會被判、會被關，後來事情過去了，組黨的名單卻越來越長。因為有人把名字加上去，大家都想搭上關鍵的列車。

各位，明天是歷史性的時刻……

（後略）

張
懋
禛

張懋禛，真光福音教會牧師

* Please turn to page 229 for English version of Joseph Chang

走進真光福音教會，大大的十字架鑲在毛玻璃上，自然光
透窗灑落，讓莊嚴氣氛又多了幾分溫暖。張懋禛牧師緩步
向前，微笑舉起彩虹旗，十字架與彩虹旗，這兩樣始終存
在疙瘩的符號於是同框。這個畫面，正好說明了他多年來
的角色，作為基督教與同志族群之間的橋樑，他是恆常難
為的夾心餅乾。

從小生長在牧師家庭，他15歲篤信耶穌，18歲在教會夏令營
中與一位弟兄互表好感，深感罪惡，兩人一起祈禱悔改。21
歲，他寫滿7張信紙，真誠地向父母自白出櫃，那一刻起，
他的人生便注定要以基督徒、同志的雙重身分進行下去。

只是，這一路上，多得是他沒料想過的困難。

不問不說，換來的牧師資格

張懋禛以成為牧師為志，進入台灣神學院就讀，卻一度被黑函攻擊，包括學
校、他所實習的教會，都收到多封傳真「舉報」他是同志，威脅神學院應將
他退學。說起往事，張懋禛已沒有太多情緒，以一貫溫柔的語調回憶，「那
個事件給了我很大的警訊：我可以成為牧師嗎？當我的身分有越來越多人
知道，我很擔心之後的發展，包括能不能順利畢業、接受長老教會的差派等
等。」潘朵拉的盒子被打開了，原先只存在於檯面下的問題，瞬間鬧得翻騰。
張懋禛原氣到想公開出櫃，被身旁好友阻止，才讓事件低調過去。「後來，
比較資深的牧師就建議我，不要找教會的工作。因為如果被差派到地方教

會，一定會有人問我感情狀況，甚至我日後跟伴侶住在一起，大家也會講話。」於是，他選擇在機構、長老教會總會工作了幾年。這段相安無事的日子沒能長久，2007 年，他申請成為正式牧師，審核過程中又是各種流言蜚語。

「長老教會審核時，有些話就傳到我耳朵裡。我知道有人提出質疑，同志能封牧嗎？滿多人反對的。後來，投票的過程裡，大家的想法是說，沒人真的來當面問過我，我也沒有公開出櫃，才能讓我通過，也很感謝一些挺同的牧師幫忙遊說。」當年台灣教會的氛圍，大概就像美國總統柯林頓面對軍中同性戀的「Don't Ask, Don't Tell」風氣，身為同性戀，要懂得低調。

面對隱藏真實自我，才換取來的牧師資格，讓張懋禛驚覺：「如果持續待在長老教會，我就得是一個在深櫃裡的牧師。」

於是，他決定開一間兼容所有人的教會，同志、跨性別，甚至是主流異性戀也好，在他眼中，所有人都值得被上帝所愛。十多年光陰，他真的做到了，真光福音教會裡，各種性／別並存，為數不少的異性戀家庭，其實也渴望找到一個能容納多元聲音的教會。

張懋禛希望從教會推起孩子的性平教育，讓這些友善的種子到各地開花，「這些孩子從小就懂得尊重不同，包括我們有跨性別的教友，他們一開始可能會懷疑，要叫叔叔或阿姨？久了也就習慣了。另外，學校的家長會也有滿多反同勢力，

163

當我們的家長進去裡面，也有機會能交流。」他用交流這個
詞，其實是經歷婚姻平權運動後的學習。

我們都是有限的人

過去的張懋禛，常對反同者感到不滿，透過參與婚權運動，
他反覆練習與異溫層的對話方式，才發現自己長期以來，累
積了太多負面情緒。「因為我本身個性沒有那麼強烈，會把
情緒壓下來，但還是會影響到自己的身心狀況，後來到一個
程度，我意識到自己不能再這樣下去。」他從同理開始，試
著思考反對者的立場，「以前會覺得他們就是食古不化、恐
同、沒有接觸新知，後來發現不見得是如此。對方可能有來
自他自己家庭、社群等等的壓力，或受到他過往生命經驗的
影響等等。」他放下論斷，承認我們都是人，都是有限的人。

回到基督教信仰的本質，人與人的關係，
人與上帝的關係，都是要有愛的。
所以當我們著重在關係上的時候，
就比較能在當中找到平衡，也能彼此了解。

「他是一個有限的人，就像我也是一個有限的人。我嘗試去
接受，他現在的狀況是這樣，我現在的狀況是這樣，怎麼找
到一個溝通點？或是，他就是反對，那我們怎麼相處下去？」
張懋禛認為，即便站在天平的兩端，也絕不能摧毀關係，「我
曾經對反對的家人有很大的情緒，後來回想自己曾經失去過
的東西，才想到，他若放下堅持，也會失去很多。」要放下
手中的東西本不容易，若身上還擔了責任，那更是困難。只
要把關係留住，未來也許還有可能找到溝通出口。

當婚姻平權運動風起雲湧，由保守教會為核心的反動勢力也
隨之集結壯大。好一陣子，同志社群視基督教為邪教，保守
基督徒更稱同志是性解放、放蕩主義分子。這種狀況讓張懋
禛很難過，「我卡在中間，這種雙重身分一開始要自處是很
難的。後來我回想，自己是怎麼認同、整合這兩個身分的？

我想，最大的原因還是『關係』。」一個對基督徒友善的同志，身邊可能有個基督徒好友；一個對同志友善的基督徒，身邊可能有個同志好友。

「回到基督教信仰的本質，人與人的關係、人與上帝的關係，都是要有愛的。所以當我們著重在關係上的時候，就比較能在當中找到平衡，也能彼此了解。」

基督教義，真的反同嗎？

許多人一定好奇，張懋禛不斷提到基督教應有的愛與包容，那為何反同者中，基督徒仍佔了人多數？甚至，還不斷強調聖經的反同立場？

〈利未記 20:13〉：「人若與男人苟合，像與女人一樣，他們二人行了可憎的事，總要把他們治死，罪要歸到他們身上。」

張懋禛說，這牽涉到不同派別對於聖經詮釋方式的不同。「老實說，這是有點麻煩的。反對的人會從字面上來理解，但正面看待的人，會認為聖經要因應不同社會背景、時代來解釋。我時常舉例，聖經以前也反對女性、支持奴隸制度，但現在我們也不認同這樣的想法了啊。」在聖經的解讀上，辯論始終存在。許多歐美的教會，花了二、三十年才從認為同性戀是罪，走到能為同志配偶證婚。要讓保守的教會轉向，不是不可能，只是需要時間。

「聖經是我們了解上帝的想法、作法，最好的準則，但它是需要人去詮釋的。很多人把焦點放在聖經怎麼說，但基督教相信的不只是聖經，基督教相信的是耶穌。」只是，在信仰耶穌的初心之外，一個主流宗教的發展，不可能缺乏組織。張懋禛認為，許多時候問題出在組織，不在教義，「倫理道德、社會規範、教會組織跟聖經的權威，這些都是比較第二層的東西。某些牧師會擔心，如果這些東西動搖了，會影響到他的權力和地位。」

他說，當一些不能理解多元的宗教人士，發現自己的話語權被挑戰，而宗教又是他的全世界時，感到恐懼也是自然的。這與教義無關，這是人性。

不完美卻重要的轉變

張懋禛一路上跟隨大平台的腳步，投入婚權運動。2016 年平權音樂會，他與 25 萬人一起站在凱道上，發現原來關心這個議題的，已經不只同志社群，感動難以言喻；2018 年公投大敗，他擔憂夥伴承受過多傷害，在教會舉辦心靈成長、壓力釋放的團體課程；2019 年立法院外，他也與大家一起見證了那歷史性的一刻，並祈禱從此之後，法律能為教會帶來改變。

「現在我發現很多基督徒可以理解，我們沒辦法要求所有人都按照基督教的倫理道德。所以有些人雖然不支持同志婚姻，但是選擇不強烈反對，或是不參與動員。因為他覺得他沒有理由因為自己的宗教觀，去阻礙這群人爭取他們應該享有的平等。」法律跨出了也許不完美、卻至關重要的一步，像初生嬰兒得經歷磕磕絆絆地學步，我們的社會也是。

接下來，張懋禎最希望看到的轉變，是所有教會都願意為同志配偶證婚，以及即使是大方出櫃的同志，也能保有擔任牧師的資格。他的 Instagram 上，與伴侶一起慶生切蛋糕，到西餐廳享受兩杯紅酒與牛排，出國旅遊時穿著同款情侶羽絨外套。這些日常那麼美好，他是一位同志、一位牧師、一位人夫，有何不可？在他眼中，每個人都應該有選擇的自由，而每個良善的選擇，都值得被深深祝福。

「什麼是 ？」Q & A

●什麼是平等？

平等就是在上帝所創造的生命中，不只是人，每個受造的生命，包括植物、動物都是平等的，應該被友善的對待。

●什麼是愛？

愛，就是愛人就像愛自己一樣。以同理心，想想看希望別人如何愛我，那我也應該如何地對待別人。

●什麼是正常？

多元就是正常，人就是獨特的，像我們每個人的指紋都不同。正常，就是去接受這個世界上有各種不同的人。

郭
媽
媽

郭媽媽，同志父母愛心協會創辦人

* Please turn to page 232 for English version of Mama Kuo

郭媽媽穿戴齊全的彩虹裝備前來，坐下後爽朗地說：「哎呀，我今天要說些不好聽的話欸，可以嗎？」得到應允後，郭媽媽約每隔十幾分鐘就會說：「同志們，你們趕快去結婚啦。」

什麼不好聽的話，原來是長輩催婚啊！

郭媽媽 2011 年成立同志父母愛心協會，她豪語至今幫出櫃的小孩零失敗，誰知最懂父母心聲、鼓勵小孩與父母對話的同志父母愛心協會，本來也只是一群聽聞孩子出櫃就躲進深櫃的脆弱爸媽。

這個世界原來有這麼多種同志啊

女兒於 15 歲出櫃，留下一張紙條後跑出家門，她嚇得不得了，馬上打電話給孩子，「不管你喜歡男生還是女生，我們都愛你，快回家吧！」回想這段反應戲稱：「也是要說場面話，嚇到孩子怎麼辦？」櫃父母剛入行，焦慮不敢說，她與先生一起上網 Google、讀一手英文資料，「一開始我們只想著安慰她，也會有點不安，她才 15 歲，那以後會變嗎？」在困惑中郭媽媽沒忘主動學習，2004 年加入同志諮詢熱線：

「我大開眼界，熊啊、猴啊還有狗……原來這個世界上存在那麼多不一樣的同志。」

無論是什麼動物，卻是同一種愛，愛子心切使她了解的同志文化比孩子更甚，「我一開始還跟她討論說妳是那種 T？那時候有鐵 T、秀氣 T 什麼的啊。我還笑她說……妳好像都不是欸，妳好邊緣喔。」也因此，郭媽媽的女兒願意主動與她分享在校園裡的戀愛煩惱：「因為她長得滿帥的，很多女孩子喜歡她，那時候還會有女孩子因為要跟她約會時間兜不攏吵架……」郭媽媽笑當時的女兒：「很需要時間管理啊。」

化身戀愛導師與她深談，甚至老師來告狀女女戀情時，郭媽媽反治其人：「那個老師很緊張，說她去學姊家過夜，他們覺得是天大的事，但我覺得，我自己以前也是住校六年，我們去外面過夜，很正常啊。」

她說自己對女兒爆棚的愛，有時候都會試圖收斂一些，免得女兒自己覺得太黏。成長路上，女兒沒這麼深入探索自己的性別認同，反倒是媽媽一頭熱栽下去。也是在那時，郭媽媽發現女兒，有可能是「跨」。

一邊問問題，一邊找答案

現在，我們必須改口稱郭媽媽的小孩為「兒子」。

「很多人問我說，他為什麼會變成一個跨性別？我覺得這是因為我們一路上看見了光譜裡有很多樣子，我也引導他思考，自己喜歡什麼樣子，我們一路去問問題，一路去找答案。」

很多人問我說，他為什麼會變成一個跨性別？我覺得這是因為我們一路上看見了光譜裡有很多樣子，我也引導他思考，自己喜歡什麼樣子，我們一路去問問題，一路去找答案。

「我知道他不喜歡自己的胸部，就有開始在找一些縮胸手術的案例……」孩子大學時初次興起手術念頭，但郭媽媽心裡也面對信仰的掙扎：「我的信仰會告訴我天主給你的東西是自然的、不可殘害自己的身體。但我後來也換個角度想，祂不會阻止人類過得幸福，如果變成自己接受的樣子是幸福的，那為什麼不呢。」

郭媽媽語帶驕傲：「兒子的變性之路，是我們一起完成的。其實過程中，他並沒有服用賀爾蒙，刻意想改變自己的聲線，或是隱瞞自己身上曾經有的女性痕跡，他身上有許多不同的特質，他不會去追求很典型的男生的樣子，那也是他。」

郭媽媽把兒子的重生視為自己的重生，再想一路走來還是有熱淚的衝動，手術的疼痛、術後的癒合，身體的疤永遠在，刻畫了生而為人「成為自己」的意志。她就像里長伯分送好消息，首當其衝跟鄰居介紹，自己的女兒現在是「兒子」了，不怕被指指點點，反而說：「我是在開他們眼界，讓他們知道，現在的世界不一樣了。」

兒子現在跟未來媳婦過著穩定的婚前生活，兩人形同步入婚姻，也即將結婚，其實早在同婚通過前，他們就已經一起買了房子。能夠與小孩一起完成人生的每個步驟，讓她感到滿足。

櫃人變貴人

不僅是自家孩子，郭媽媽這幾年來也看顧了許多同志的出櫃、與櫃父母攜手走過，也因此她更明白「櫃人」變「貴人」的喜悅。

不把這一路看作奉獻，而是學習：

「天主賜給我一個特殊的小孩，讓我有這樣子的機會去服務別人，要不然我可能現在每天只是在家吃胖胖無所事事。」

幾年來不缺席運動與家庭現場，郭媽媽的最大任務，是化解反同方、父母們的憂慮與憤怒。2018 年公投綁大選，反同方與挺同方各自奔走，郭媽媽在那年因為壓力過大罹患顏面神經失調：「那個過程真的很痛苦，因為真的很希望衝人數，我每天晚上睡覺時都在想要怎麼跟他們說，今天有哪一句話，我是不是可以講得更好？我方要怎麼進步到有那個力量去跟宗教體系對話……」

面對面的對話交鋒，有時傷人，多半無解。遭逢公投的票數差距，失望自然是有，不過作為大人，郭媽媽不厭其煩接起同志小孩的電話：「孩子希望我們幫忙去說服爸媽，又偏偏那些爸媽可能是教會裡的牧師牧師娘，那種對話，通常都會比較尖銳，他們會拿聖經裡的教義給你看，有些問題，你真的也會答不上來。」

「我後來發現最大的差異就是，我是同志的父母，我認識了那麼多的同志，我去講，講的是『人』的故事，但他們講的是『神』的故事。」

連續幾個月的折磨，問她怎麼撐下來，她又不以為苦，「我們看的路會比較長，像是現在婚姻平權過了，其實還有好多事要做。」

「當然也有非常令人高興的案例，很多成功和解的家庭。父母多半很想了解，但是通常……小孩都比較看不起父母，我有很多案例，小孩覺得父母不懂。但我到現場，發現他們是多麼地愛孩子啊，只是缺乏資訊，在我所認識的父母裡，為了小孩什麼都願意學。」

郭媽媽看許多在外面能幹的同志，回到家卻不見得有論述自己的能力：「接受自己以外，也要接受爸媽，用愛牽引爸媽一起往前。我也是普通的平凡人，如果沒有我的小孩，我不會認識這個世界那麼多。這些爸媽，都有可能是別人的貴人，因為認識自己的小孩，可以去跟街上的阿桑、三姑六婆說，就有更多人能認識這個世界。」

同志父母愛心協會存在的必要，在於不斷接觸社會階層裡的經濟中堅，「我們在努力接觸那些異性戀、有年紀有能力有權力的人、制定法律的人。」同志影響父母、父母影響家族，她鼓勵同志們像她一樣「拋頭露面」站出來，讓社會知道，我們在這裡。

快去結婚吧

從成立至今，同志父母愛心協會的路數一致，透過民間遊說讓更多父母接受同志。「我曾經遇到一個人跟我說，某某人的小孩是同志，她好像過得很慘。我當下就回他說，你認識她嗎？她並不慘，她很快樂，過得多好啊。這個社會一直誤以為，只要是同志，就會不幸。我們很需要更多幸福的版本啊。」

這時，郭媽媽又使出催婚技能：「專法通過後，第一年結婚是三千多對，接下來是兩千多對，然後疫情，會不會又更慘啊？以前累積的都已經出清了⋯⋯」她一個個問我們為什麼還不結婚？語重心長：「我們要建立一種文化，去相信說結婚是好的，甚至有小孩也是好的。」

「婚權通過以後，其實父母更容易接受小孩是同志，他們知道可以結婚，至少心裡是有安全感的。不只是父母需要了解更多小孩的同志生活、交往對象，社會也需要看到更多結婚幸福的同志家庭，我們才能推動更多後面所需要的東西啊，生養小孩、人工生殖⋯⋯」郭媽媽期待同志婚姻能帶來顛覆性別角色的家庭樣本：「以前社會有很多家庭性別角色分工，但同志家庭根本不需要這些，家務的分擔可以更均衡，各自做自己擅長的事，這難道不會是比現在異性戀結婚更棒的地方嗎？」

過去，同志並不將結婚視為一個選項，郭媽媽說，現在已經突破萬難地讓同志可以結婚了：「你們可以更勇敢，快去結婚吧。」

你們可以更勇敢，
快去結婚吧！

175

「什麼是 ？」Q & A

●什麼是善良？

把你的生活過好，然後希望別人也過好，我覺得這就是從善的出發，每個人都可以值得過更好的生活，一點點付出也可能引發他人價值觀的改變。

●什麼是愛？

愛是責任，也是忍耐，在愛中兩個人會牽絆在一起也會有妥協，這種妥協裡會激發你很大的成長，在相處中會從這個人身上有所學習，關係是需要調（ㄊㄧㄠˊ）整（ㄐㄧㄠˋ）的，像我們家掌廚的是我老公，我都會跟他說「你要負責我吃飯超過九十歲唷」。

♥ 同場加映郭媽媽的出櫃保證班 SOP ♥

首先當然是不要跟父母搞壞關係！不要想說三年都沒回家、沒聯絡，那怎麼可能成功？接下來按照步驟：

第一，敘述發現的時機與狀態；
第二，分享確認的契機與心情；
第三，細數同志大事記，交往過的對象、參與過的同志場合；
第四，分享現在的交友狀態（建議在有另一半的狀況講，失戀非好時機）；
第五，分享自己未來想過的日子，要跟誰過？養貓還是養小孩？父母最擔心的，是你未來沒有一個家。出櫃不是科學，同步自己與父母的時間軸，才能讓父母理解自己的心理與掙扎。

希望大家都能在愛你與你愛的人面前，快樂做自己。

温
貞
菱

温貞菱，演員

* Please turn to page 236 for English version of Chen-Ling Wen

「大雨之下，我們一起撐起一片彩虹。能一起走到現在，還會一起走到永遠。國際不再恐同日的好消息，人人生而平等的權利，可以結婚了。Let's get married.＃全濕回家熱水澡」

2019 年 5 月 17 日的 Instagram 照片裡，溫貞菱在立法院外摟著好友姚愛寗，兩位氣質空靈的女藝人，頭髮濕搭搭地黏在額間，卻仍笑得開懷，眼睛瞇成一線。溫貞菱第一次公開表態支持婚姻平權，是在 2016 年左右，婚權運動最熱的這三年，她幾乎無役不與。原以為她過去就對同志平權議題有所關注，沒想到答案卻是否定的，她說，在接觸婚權運動之前，她甚至不認為這是個「議題」。

為什麼不能喜歡同性？

「我剛開始參與時，是非常樂觀的。就星座來講，可能是比較夢幻泡泡的一個雙魚座的世界，一切都很美好。之後才透過上街、參與活動慢慢靠近現實，發現原來我的想法，與社會上某些人有非常嚴重的出入。」這權利那麼基本，只要大家一起把聲音傳達給政府，就會有所改變了吧？當時未滿 25 歲的溫貞菱是這麼想的。

情欲萌發的國、高中青春期，她早已習慣身邊的女同學牽著女朋友，自己也曾在 17 歲時被女生吸引過。「當時，我也並不覺得我的性傾向有問題。我一直沒有辦法明白，為什麼這樣是不好或是不對；反過來說，無法理解不同性傾向這件事，反倒讓我覺得比較奇怪。」她說，自己直到現在，還是偶爾會被某些同性朋友吸引，「那個喜歡的程度會不會到愛情，就是另一回事了。」她無法想像有人會反對同志，第一次在路上看到有人舉著反同的標語，還心想：「他會不會是不知道自己舉的是什麼？」

這份天真並不無用，經過幾年歷練、實際參與運動，她得以重新反思這份理所當然。

「我這麼理所當然地站在我覺得正確的位子上，或許他們也是這麼理所當然地站在他們覺得正確的位子上。」

她回看同志運動的歷史，認為時間終能帶領我們向前，「同志運動剛開始那時，我甚至還沒出生吧。所以只要每個人慢慢運用自身影響力去溝通，持續做，我相信這件事情會越來越好。」她回憶起自己在俄羅斯讀書時的經驗，她與一個當地女孩聊到自己很支持婚姻平權，沒想到對方卻很不能理解，「她 19 歲，從沒在莫斯科的路上看過任何同志。我才想起大學時有人和我說過，如果同志在俄羅斯街頭表現親密，是可能被打的。」

溫貞菱回台半年，某日卻突然收到那位女孩的簡訊，「她很興奮地說，剛剛在酒吧遇見人生中第一個男同志，她還和對方聊天。」因為社會封閉，遇見同志竟然成為如此獵奇的體驗。「我覺得我很幸運，我很早就有那個環境和機會，讓我認知這件事，不像她到成年後，甚至都還沒看過、不太理解這個族群。」對溫貞菱而言，

我這麼理所當然地站在我覺得正確的位子上，或許他們也是這麼理所當然地站在他們覺得正確的位子上。

支持同志平權不是選擇，而是像到學校交朋友那樣自然發生。
她認為，擁有這份認知是幸運的。

戰い，繼續戰鬥吧！

「我希望在我 25 歲之前，可以看到台灣第一對同志伴侶結婚。」

2017 年，溫貞菱以《最後的詩句》獲得第 52 屆金鐘獎迷你劇
集／電視電影女主角獎，站上台，她開口便先說了這句話。
身為公眾人物，溫貞菱從不避諱表達立場，即使她深知社會
上有一大群人與她持相反意見。而這些人有可能是她的觀眾，
不是嗎？

「我相信，即使是跟一個你深愛的人，你們之間都有許多事
要磨合。你不可能跟一個人全然地一拍即合，有很多觀念、
思想是需要對話的。」抱持著這樣的心念，她不擔心粉絲因
此退粉，反倒渴望對話的機會。「我的確收過很多批評的言
論，甚至有人說：『這麼支持，妳是 T 吧？』但這反倒讓我
想更用力支持。」她時常告訴自己不要感到受傷，因為同志
朋友可是一直在面對類似傷害。

「性傾向或是性別不被認同的人，從一出生開始，應該是無

時無刻都在受傷。因此，每次收到想傷害我的評論，我都會
更心疼一直以來在異樣眼光下活著的同志們。」

2018 年公投大敗，她也是用這樣的心情撐了過來。「那時回
家先哭了一下，但很快就平復下來，因為當你覺得這就是結
果，容易沒什麼希望。我馬上開始關注大家對事件的反應，
發了一些文去鼓勵朋友，希望大家相信還是有機會往我們想
要的方向前進。」那份再站起來的力量，還是來自於心疼，「如
果我現在受傷，那同志朋友怎麼辦？」雖說如此，她並不認
為自己是在為「他人」爭取權益。

「我不會去劃分我們、他們，我會覺得，在支持婚姻平權的
同時，是在支持自己的權利、未來小孩的權利，或許你現在
不會知道，但它可能是你身邊任何一個人的權利。」

專法或許不是最完美的解答，但已是足以慶賀的一道雨後彩虹。溫貞菱明白這條路還沒到盡頭，但就如她在 2019 年 5 月 17 日那天所說，她想一起走到永遠。「我最近有點迷上《進擊的巨人》，『戰い！（讀音：Tatakai）』繼續戰鬥吧。社會有許多事情值得我們去理解、去學習、去改變。我會希望，自己在這個過程中，能夠跟著所有人往更好的地方去。」戰い，倒了再站起來，別忘了，我們都不是一個人。

『戰い』繼續續戰鬥吧。
社會有許多事情值得我們去理解、去學習、去改變
我會希望，自己在這個過程中，
能夠跟著所有人往更好的地方去。

「什麼是 ？」Q & A

●什麼是善良？

亞當‧斯密說，遵從自己的心、做利他的行為，這就是最大的善良。我支持同婚運動的想法也是如此。

●什麼是愛？

愛就是，希望自己所愛的人幸福，並不吝嗇給予、真心不求回報。

●什麼是正常？

不理解的時候，可能會覺得某些人是不正常的。但是世界很大，有很多不同的人，這才是正常的。不應該因為不理解而想去調整別人。

李
芝
晨

李芝晨，時為婚姻平權大平台台南組織專員、現為不動產經紀人

* Please turn to page 238 for English version of Chih Chen Li

在同志運動裡，有些名字不一定會被推到最前面，但他們卻仍然站在前線。「我看到名單擺開來，想說找我訪問好嗎……」李芝晨曾為婚姻平權大平台的台南專員，訪問前她思量許久，決定受訪，是希望同志運動的痛苦與榮耀，不要少了地方的視野。

近期剛考過駕照的李芝晨，新手上路，方才停了一會車才進來，雖然年輕，但掌舵的架式並不生疏，學生時期就已投入性別運動的她氣場強，一坐下來就是放鬆氣氛，業務的體貼性格，自然地從頭道來。

2018 年，李芝晨就坐在這裡，一個人擔綱雲嘉南的運動部署，從召集志工到培訓，都起源於依傍在台南新芽協會辦公室的　方小小工作桌。

一個異性戀的政治啟蒙

李芝晨投注社運的政治路線，並非一開始就關懷同志。「我小時候因為受到我爸的影響，是超恐同的人……」爸爸是地方人士，家裡是做生意的地方，一個茶桌接待許多來往的鄰居，茶桌上的長輩們看到馬英九會嘲諷「同性戀，娘娘腔，話都講不好」，那是一個沒人在意什麼是「性別氣質」的時代。「以前看到青峰廣告代言果汁，看到他喝完發出『啊～』的聲音，我爸會罵說『死腳仔』，我也會跟著他說。我以前從來不會想像到，我的身邊可能存在同志，又加上我們是在南部，就算有，可能也不敢出櫃。」

2001 年，柯一正所執導、改編杜修蘭小說的《逆女》是她第一次認識同志。

《逆女》作為台灣第一個女同志電視劇,與 2003 年的文學改
編電視劇《孽子》所記錄的台灣特定時空下的同志敘事,建
構山當時同性戀主體性與政治意識,「我因此有興趣,還去
借書,懵懵懂懂地認識了『同志』這個角色。」高中讀女校,
她旁觀帥學姐與正學姐萌發戀情,「那時候都覺得,以後她
們可能還是會交男朋友吧。」

高中畢業那年,由學生組織發起的反媒體壟斷運動以維護台
灣新聞自由提出訴求,李芝晨受到啟蒙,「那時候就是一個
昌粉,會自己爬文很多資料……大學我讀的剛好跟行政公共
事務有關,系上老師很支持我們去認識這些議題。」2014 年
3 月 18 日,青年們經歷一場精神至肉身的流血,「晚安台灣」
是每個人睡前在心裡默念的砥礪與溫柔。李芝晨也去到現場,
見證了一整個時代的鬆動。

2015 年逢總統大選前,許多第三勢力開始成立,台灣兩黨獨
大的時代變動在即,「那時候欣潔代表社民黨出來參選,我
遠遠地看著就覺得她是一個女神般的存在……」而後,李芝
晨認識了以綠社盟參政的楊智達,楊智達的身分為同志,開
啟了她關注性別運動的契機。

原來我的發文,會影響其他生命

2016 年的大選,李芝晨在苗博雅的團隊擔任選舉志工,「後
來我也當智達的志工,越當越深入,智達會笑說我根本是辦
公室主任。他們都是公開出櫃的同志候選人,因為我想在這

場選舉運動貢獻，自然會去了解如何對外論述他們的身分。」一起跑選舉，自然也見證了社會的差別待遇，南部選民的差辱常見，也曾有直接把文宣丟回志工臉上的情況。

「當時我是憤青一枚，我會在臉書發很多憤青文，臉友們也陸續知道我的政治傾向，有人會來跟我說，因為我的發言跟社會氛圍，讓他們更敢出櫃。」

原來一個異性戀的「友善」可以如此切實地影響其他生命。她的社群同溫層，漸形 60% 以上都是同志。

「2018 年，台南要辦一個同志遊行，當時是第 3 屆，但台南一直都沒有很大的運動組織，就以『台南彩虹遊行聯盟』為名，智達做總召，我也去當幹部。」從路權申請到志工統籌，正式入坑。接續聽聞 2018 年的公投消息，在楊智達引薦下認識呂欣潔，決定參與 2018 公投的地方部署，成為婚姻平權大平台的台南專員。

地方的公投動起來

彼時台中、台南、高雄各有一名專員負責區域統籌，「因為那年下修成 18 歲可以有公投資格，是我覺得可以開始跑到街上發文宣的時候，但在 2018 年中，傳統媒體根本不關注，在街頭怎麼喊都沒有人關心。」

在無人發聲之處發聲，正是拓荒者的使命。越接近年底公投，光是擴散組織、要物資、生場地就忙到地老天荒，也去拜訪地方候選人、連結地方關注議題的組織。

「時間越接近，大家的情緒跟焦慮越多，我很像是一個官方窗口角色，也要承接地方志工的聲音，他們會覺得地方的資源總是慢一些，希望自己可以更出力，我每兩週一次到台北開會，也會去分享。」南北距離，可以動員的能量、能運用的資源都有限，然而，我們都記得 2016 那年開始每當發出凱道召集令，地方的遊覽車一台一台包車上來的情景，沒有這種意願，不會創下 25 萬人挺同志的現場。在有限的資源下打效能最大值的戰，每個人都並不容易。

從打點、擺攤、找志工、辦講座、擴散文宣，土法煉鋼地推動運動氣氛，「台南的組織力量，其實並不是來自立案組織，大多是來自性別友善的店家。」一間間親臨拜訪，從文青書店與咖啡店、到傳統餐廳與地方小吃都掛上彩虹旗、挺同志，當年，他們在三百家挺同志的小店掛上了彩虹。

身為一個異性戀，在參與同志運動時不免遭受質疑，有時遇

到超過親密界限的同志志工，李芝晨也會擔心自己傷害對方而不敢明言。接近公投時，一個志工在街頭發文宣受拒，李芝晨事後關心，志工卻回她：「是啦，反正這個公投結果怎樣也不關你這個異性戀的事。」

「我懂她的情緒，但我那時候真的傷得很重。」難免情緒張力，婚姻平權大平台設立督導制度，關心夥伴的心理健康。不過那時，她總是把自己放得比較後面，因為站在領導位置，需要大量照顧他人情緒，公投開票的晚上，台北與各地連線，視訊即時開票，「當時公投的狀態加上韓國瑜，我覺得大家情緒都很崩潰，那天我們就在這邊喝小酒、彈吉他，大家團聚在一起度過。」

當時各群組傳出沮喪的同志朋友找不到人，她一心想著：「大家真的很努力了，不要下車。」

讓媽媽拾起腐心

李芝晨說話很有條理，承襲做房仲的母親，她在 2018
年公投結束後返回職場，那也是放下運動傷害、重新出
發。先是一起在同志運動路上打開「家」的定義，兜售
房子也遇過一起看房的同志伴侶。從家到房子，收容了
她倡議與溝通的掙扎，不僅是面向社會，也面向自己的
家庭。

在她從事運動的時間裡，不時會有些同志出版物寄到家
裡，「搞不好我爸一直以為我是還沒出櫃的同志。」
雖從未正面談論，不時在 LINE 指證假新聞與政治不正
確，古板的爸爸也漸漸受到女兒的影響，甚至在公投時
支持同志。

在李芝晨跑公投那一年，媽媽身體發生狀況，沒有大量
陪伴在媽媽身邊，反而造成不諒解，一面有個投入同志
運動的女兒，一面在教會受到反同思想影響，公投前一
天，媽媽雖然沒有允諾李芝晨期望的投票法，但最終選
擇不領公投票。

不過自從楊智達結婚了，開始有更多改變，「他們婚禮
辦得很盛大，我跟我媽還一起討論說要包多少給他……
很感謝有他這樣一位好友，讓我媽媽可以看到同志的面
貌就是這麼生活化、這麼貼近我們每個人。」媽媽在女
兒言談間經常聽聞同志好友的婚姻生活，也漸漸放下心
防。最近他們一起看了《如果 30 歲還是處男，似乎就

我覺得這都是機會，
她也跟我一起看得很入戲。
我媽看到安達清被黑澤優一摸頭時，
她還盒說，哎情好可愛哦。

能成為魔法師》，媽媽表示：「這個是男主角？啊這個也是男主角喔？啊這個是比較像楊智達的嗎？」

「我覺得這都是機會，她也跟我一起看得很入戲。我媽看到安達清被黑澤優一摸頭時，她還會說，哎呀好可愛哦。」

腐心被激發，媽媽也慢慢視此為正常。當李芝晨重新回到家庭，和解也有了可能。如今感謝楊智達與洪國峰、安達清被黑澤優一摸頭，腐力散播，魔法充滿——大街小巷，看見了更多「家」的形態。

「什麼是 ？」Q & A

●什麼是正常？

在沒有傷害他人的情況下，不管我是否喜歡，只要你喜歡，那都是正常。

●什麼是愛？

像剛剛說有些家庭衝突是不是需要修復？我跟媽媽每天都有大大小小的衝突，但我們也持續溝通，這樣共處到下一個明天，即使衝突，我們知道一覺醒來，還是要一起吃早餐。這就是愛吧。

THE EMERGENCY MEETINGS—REVISITED

台灣同志運動,最早可回推至 80 年代,但 2016 到 2019 這短短幾年的大步邁進,對同運團體而言,絕對是極為關鍵的光榮戰役。

2019 年,台灣成為全亞洲第一個承認同性婚姻的國家。催生《司法院釋字第 748 號解釋施行法》的背後,是各路同運、婦運團體取得最大共識的民主練習。包括台灣同志諮詢熱線協會、婦女新知基金會、台灣同志家庭權益促進會等,以婚姻平權大平台之名作為整合及號召,團結一致才看見了曙光。

當然,這一路走來必有磕磕碰碰。局勢及風向瞬息萬變,身上背負著來自團體內外期待與壓力的他們,數不清幾個夜裡,撐住沉重的眼皮,「緊急會議」直到深夜。在同婚通過兩年後的今天,他們再次聚首,回憶來時的路,重返緊急會議。

參與人員:

彩虹平權大平台:呂欣潔、鄧筑媛、曹承羲(美克)、郭宜婷
台灣同志諮詢熱線協會:彭治鏐(夜盲)・副秘書長、杜思誠(小杜)・政策推廣部主任
婦女新知基金會:曾昭媛・資深研究員、林實芳・董事
台灣同志家庭權益促進會:蔡尚文・前副理事長
同志人權法案遊說聯盟:蘇珊(Cindy)・執行長
GagaOOLala:林志杰(Jay)・創辦人

* Please turn to page 243 for English version

場景一

台灣能順利推動同婚專法，婚姻平權大平台（現：彩虹平權大平台）的整合與推動功不可沒。雖然「大平台」這個神秘的詞彙，至今語意不明（？），但用在婚姻平權的推動上卻意外合適：這是一群滿滿的人、滿滿的各路團體，用滿滿的愛創建的大平台！

雖然婚權只是同志權益中的一小部分，來自四方的同運、婦運團體，卻願意攜手找出最大公約數，在每個意見相左的時刻異中求同。而他們最初究竟是如何把手牽在一起呢？

Q：最初如何確立要全力以「婚權」為目標出發，各團體又如何整合資源？

欣潔：欸，我們當初到底怎麼成立這個團體的（完全失憶）？

眾人七嘴八舌：好像是尤辦找的吧？

昭媛：我來說明一下，我跟筑媛之前是尤美女委員的助理，我是從2019……欸不是，哈哈哈（尚文表示：你是想下班了是不是？），2012年到2015年這段時間，那在此前後都是在婦女新知工作，所以跟尤是很認識的。

2016年婚姻平權大平台組成前夕，尤正好就任第二任立委，因為上一任沒辦法通過婚權法案，立法院又有「屆期不連續原則」，得重新提案。2013年伴侶盟請鄭麗君提案，尤是共同提案人。2016年2月立院新的任期開始，尤私下詢問鄭麗君是否再次提案，知道她已準備520要去擔任文化部長。因在2014年時，鄭的版本被反同方說要修太多法條、浪費資源，尤就順勢決定要重寫，那要自己寫的話，新的草案要跟哪些同志團體合作？大家就展開討論，簡單講是這樣（尚文：你從沒簡單講過好嗎）。

欣潔：那 Cindy 跟 Jay 是怎麼加入的啊？誰問你們要不要來開會的？

Cindy：我這邊也是尤辦找的。

Jay：我記得很清楚，是欣潔來酷摩沙獎時，問我要不要加入，那時尤美女委員也有說要不要一起全力以赴。

欣潔：喔喔喔，我想起來那個畫面！

Jay：呵呵呵，妳可能那時候喝太多酒了。

欣潔：那天的確是喝了不少……後來，我們好像是為了要線上募款，才想說要來取個名字？

昭媛：對，要線上募資才開始討論，要有什麼聯盟的名字。在此之前我們大型集會都是各個民間團體聯合。

欣潔：因為我們每個團體的名字都很長，我每次都要唸好長一串，也不能全都放上去，但什麼資訊站、聯盟好像都很無聊，陣線也有人用過了。那時剛好王大陸講「大平台」，我們網站工程師是個年輕男孩，他就說最近大平台很夯，點擊率會上升，後來就真的這樣取了（笑）。

場景二

2016 年底，婚姻平權大平台成員逐步到齊，與尤辦共同討論的條文也告一段落。考量當時社會氛圍還算祥和，反同方並沒有過於激烈的言論或行為；加上蔡英文總統也在就任前承諾推動婚姻平權，他們對於法案推動並不急躁，原訂在 2017 農曆新年過後的會期提出。

沒想到，台大教授畢安生卻在 2016 年同志大遊行前夕墜樓身亡，同志社群一片譁然，也引發社會關注同性伴侶的權益問題。同時，國民黨新任立委許毓仁在政論節目上公開表示將提出婚姻平權法案，讓民進黨非常著急。

Q：聽說原本希望在 2017 年才提案修法，為何選在 2016 年緊急提案？

昭媛：當時大家條文討論得差不多，尤美女正好也有抽到召委，但還沒討論倡議策略，也沒那麼急。

夜盲：我記得我們原本是決定 2017 年再進去。我覺得後來發生畢安生老師的事件，是啟動的關鍵。

小杜：嗯，剛好是遊行前發生。又因為蔡英文當選前，有公開表示要支持同性婚姻，整體輿論是有利的。

實芳：（試圖發言但麥克風完全沒聲音。）

欣潔：啊啊，實芳妳要說什麼？

實芳：不好意思，這樣有了嗎？我記得還有一件事，是許毓仁上了「有話好說」，公開說要提案。我們就跟民進黨說：「你們如果不先提，讓國民黨先提會非常非常難看。」

昭媛：對，因為蔡英文有政治承諾，民進黨就有壓力，要趕在許毓仁之前提案。尤就找了很多立委連署，開記者會宣布要正式提案。

夜盲：記得那時尤委員還有找我們去開會，當下就做了決定說，提吧。

尤美女立委提案後，於 2016 年 11 月 17 日召開「立法院司法及法制委員會」討論法條，反同方卻大動作登報號召民眾集結包圍立法院，下跪、翻牆樣樣來，甚至有人透過熟識立委助理帶領潛入會議，激烈行為與言論，威脅尤委員的人身安全。最終，尤委員在保全人員的護送下緊急離開現場。

當天，大平台成員聚集在慕哲咖啡觀看會議轉播，發現反同方的行為完全出乎意料，除了感到委屈，也心疼尤委員的遭遇，不少人因而落下淚來。這次事件，戳破了他們的粉紅泡泡，原來，即使在總統表態、社會輿論有利，如此順風的狀況下，前方的路，也將是荊棘滿布。

Q：2016 年 11 月 17 日當天，尤美女主持委員會審查法案時，遭遇反同方強烈抗議，你們如何因應？

欣潔：我記得，我們有決定審查那天不要做集會？……等一下，我覺得鄧筑媛的臉好好笑，妳是不是什麼都不記得？

夜盲：我覺得大家會覺得這邊是一群喝茫的人在討論！（爆笑）

昭媛：那時是說，因為尤美女是主席，不要太過刺激反同方，不要有大型集會。

實芳：因為反同方在那之前沒有大動作過，即使有真愛聯盟、1130 凱道的集會之類的……

昭媛：對，就是沒有什麼馬路下跪那種。

小杜：那時候大家其實覺得社會普遍支持，為了不要有太多社會對立，讓政府也覺得這個法案是可以通過，不太有爭議。

夜盲：對，所以我們不知道反同的抗議行動會這麼……極端？

實芳：因為政府也確實覺得棘手，我們之前的討論是，希望是低調的、偷偷讓它過去，後來才發現不可能，哈哈哈。

欣潔：我們那天是在慕哲咖啡？尚文去上班了？Jay 有來嗎？

尚文：我一直都在上班好嗎！

Jay：我應該是帶團隊去立院現場拍攝。

昭媛：對，我們租場地在那邊看畫面，他們闖進去，狂拍委員會的大門。就是看起來很不理性，大聲咆哮：「尤美女放過我們！」

Cindy：我們在慕哲，我記得尤辦助理跟許毓仁都會一直跟我們講發生什麼事。我們很怕反同方衝進去傷害尤，沒有意料到他們會到肢體。

實芳：因為那天本來沒有預料會有反同方，所以反同方的訊息一直進來我就覺得好混亂喔！加上那天咖啡店的測試非、常、走，我們在地下室。常常都想說，啊現在到哪裡了？我怎麼都聽不到（笑）？

欣潔：對，委員打來我們也常常接不到。我記得當時尤委員跟 Jason（許毓仁）都打來問能不能開公聽會，我們是堅持不要。後來審查被迫結束後，媒體一直問我們反應，我們才決定要在中興大樓的空地開記者會，偷偷摸摸從慕哲回到立法院，走後門，因為很怕遇到反同方、被攻擊。記得還一直有網友問要不要衝？反同都衝了我們不衝？

實芳：那是一個從來不會有人開記者會的地方，鎮江街跟中興大樓後門交叉口。反同方牧師還跑來叫囂，反正是很瘋狂的一天。

欣潔：對，他叫什麼？我已經不記得了，什麼格伯拉底？蘇格拉底？之類的（笑）。

夜盲：忻底波拉！反正就是他認出我們，叫囂了一番。

欣潔：那天大家的心情是什麼？還記得嗎？

昭媛：我們一堆人都哭了，大家自己承認吧！

夜盲：現在想起來會覺得錯估了局勢判斷。不曉得對方會這麼激烈，很受傷吧，因為我們原本以為可以順順通過，結果還被妥協要加開兩場公聽會，有被欺負的感覺。後來我居然看到曾昭媛哭了……

昭媛：是你先哭的吧！

夜盲：好啦，我承認我先哭的好不好。

欣潔：他們兩位其實是比較絕情的人，沒看過他們哭！

夜盲：一部分也是心疼尤委員啦。

Cindy：對，我們也很怕反同方去傷害她。那種不理性有嚇到我們，會怕變成激烈的兩方對話。

夜盲：我們從來沒遇過反同人士會用肢體。

欣潔：因為他們以前不敢碰到同性戀啊，可能覺得碰到也會變成同性戀。他們以前會圍人，但不會爬牆啊！

場景三

司法及法制委員會決議此案需召開兩場公聽會之後再議。在意外觸發反同方新技能後，大平台成員全體覺醒，決定接下來要在不正面衝突的前提下大量集會，凝聚挺同方的向心力，也讓社會大眾看見輸人不輸陣的氣勢。

Q：經過反同方的驚魂記之後，你們如何擬定策略，進行下一步行動？

欣潔：美克會進來工作，就是因為，呵呵呵，我們討論之後每一場都要集會，要把場地都佔下來。

尚文：對，我們決定，不要正面對決，但要集會。

昭媛：真的是因為 11 月 17 日反同行動激烈，我們覺得之後的街頭造勢也一定要相當，光靠在立法院的席次不足夠。

美克：我就是那時被找進來，因為他們說「接下來有密集動員的可能」，但剛開始都是非專職的人力，考慮到如果要有很多積極動員，會很難做起來。

實芳：（麥克風依然很小聲）喂？喂？這樣聽得到嗎？我記得那時我們有把日曆列出來，看看哪幾天有可能審查，呵呵呵，一定要全部借到。

筑媛：12 月 3 日反同在凱道大集結，我們就決定要在他們後面，剛好 12 月 10 日是世界人權日，才有了那場 25 萬人音樂會。

夜盲：因為他們辦完，社群都很生氣。

美克：我們的準備是，有一場他們的活動，就再接我們的活動。為了避免正面衝突，如果要辦活動，要把周邊全部借起來，比方辦在青島東路，中山南路、林森、濟南路也會借。那時大家的身分證字號都借我，12 點一到就準時開始搶場地。

欣潔：但辦活動突然要花很多錢，那時像 Jay、Cindy 都有幫忙募很多款。我們這種小 NGO 真的有點撐不了。

美克：我記得那時我把預算列出來後，Jay、Cindy 看一看就說，嗯，他們去想個辦法。然後第一場的一百萬就出來了。

欣潔：超級可靠！

小杜：我覺得那時候有那麼多人幫忙，反同團體也是幫我們宣傳很多，因為他們造謠、買廣告，假訊息一大堆，弄到連異性戀朋友都覺得很荒謬。

欣潔：那時 Jay 你去募款，大家的反應是怎樣？

Jay：我覺得大家有意識到，同志團體已經火力全開。我跟 Cindy 的方向是，先找年紀比較大的有孩子的同志家長，他們有累積了一些財富，很願意提供。也找娛樂圈的大哥大姐，也許不願意公開名字，但都很大方，十萬、十五萬在給，還滿順利的。

場景五

Q：2018 年初，反同方提出公投案，當時你們經過哪些討論？最終為何決定以挺同公投應對？

欣潔：公投這件事，其實我們一開始只想要推「三個不同意」，結果面臨其他人提出挺同公投……這個過程，呃，大家記得我們是怎麼決定要一起推動「兩好三壞」的嗎？

小杜：因為大平台有諮詢其他國際組織，美國 Freedom to Marry 的人跟我們分享，遇到公投這種訊息很複雜的，最好讓大家很明確地知道要投什麼，所以策略上只要「三個不同意」就好。結果後來又多出兩個同意案，只好改成推「兩好三壞」。

欣潔：那時大家的心情是怎樣？

夜盲：那時候最有情緒應該是妳吧（笑）！我記得妳有去跟苗博雅討論？

欣潔：對啊，我有去找他們討論啊，是邀請他們來熱線聊聊，當時有幾位夥伴也有一起。阿苗在社群上說要發起挺同公投，我們希望說服他們不要繼續，但當時來討論的阿苗、溫朗東等等網路意見領袖就說，希望是讓民眾決定這件事。

昭嬡：因為釋憲已經站在同志這邊，所以反同方才很急，想透過公投翻案。但其實策略上只要等立法院通過，或是釋憲的兩年期限到就好。

欣潔：對，所以我們認為在設定策略的邏輯上發起公投不合理，但阿苗應該是一個熱血，貼文已經出去了，因為沒有事先討論過這個方式，當時確實非常措手不及。

實芳：最後為了團體和諧，民眾也會來問，大家就還是投入收連署書，沒有避掉。這兩個公投成案後才決定變成「兩好三壞」的方向。

欣潔：公投結果，我們不驚訝。11 月中我們就看過民調，但太慘了，我們當時也不太確定這結果是不是真的，也在想民調會不會不準啊（笑），也有諮詢政治學教授，大家都說不太合理。後來討論很久，才決定先不要公布。

夜盲：我們做了 3 次民調。

欣潔：7 月、9 月民調都是五五波，11 月中的最後一個民調直接降 20%。

夜盲：後來覺得應該是因為反方是用全國選戰規模在做廣告的。

實芳：他們有幾支 30 秒的廣告，廣告露出頻率遠高於我們，但我們募來的款項要下廣告、置入常被拒絕。

尚文：像我們幾個月前下訂某電視台的時段，到 10 月底，他們卻說董事會決議不接受播出，就沒了。

欣潔：連有些客運廣告也被拒絕。

小杜：其實確定公投成案之後，我們就在想要做些什麼，包括電話諮詢等等。因為反同公投一定會讓同志朋友情緒大受影響。

夜盲：後來結果出來，連我自己都可以感受到心理狀況受影響。熱線有串聯各地同志組織，辦一些友善的活動，因為很多同志朋友的狀況很差。

欣潔：我們當下看到開票結果差不多了之後，就有馬上討論，如果很難過很悲傷，社群好像會覺得沒救了。「還是要有希望」、「我們不會放棄」，是我們作為運動者負責的態度。

場景六

公投大敗，大平台仍抱著希望向前，不斷為專法條文爭取更多空間。終於，2019 年 5 月 17 日，立法院拍板通過《司法院釋字第748 號解釋施行法》，眾人在滂沱大雨下隔著雨衣互相擁抱、感動落淚，天空竟也好似看見了這份喜悅，瞬間畫出一道彩虹。

相較於大眾的激動，二年多來承擔大部分壓力與責任，早已習慣公事公辦、喜怒不形於色的大平台成員，當下或許比較想好好睡上一覺。只是，這份感動不是不到，而是時候未到。當他們轉身回到各自的生活中時，總在不經意的細節裡感受到自己的努力有多美好。

美克參加第一場同志友人的婚禮時，看見朋友與伴侶、雙方父母一起站在台上時，感動得亂七八糟，「原來我真的改變了他們的生命，改變了台灣。這件事好棒、好美。」尚文則在經過這幾年的洗禮後，發現努力建立和維繫「願意溝通」的形象的艱難與重要，「我必須承認，很多時候我都不想跟無理的反方溝通，但基於大平台的形象、立場必須去做，事後看來這是最大的成長。」

實芳、昭媛事隔兩年再回憶，深刻體會到，當每個人都願意投入自身微小的力量，能創造出無限的可能。「很多人用自己的生命在影響社會，包括有大法官的學生決定跟老師出櫃等等，這些善意所激起的漣漪很讓我感動。」實芳這麼說。而參與婦運幾十年的昭媛，說自己從沒遇過這麼多人願意投入的運動，「過去常常只有團體間互相連署。這對我來說是感動也是學習。在運動中，我們如何讓更多人願意貢獻力量？」

為募款貢獻良多的 Jay，認為自己親眼見證了民主社會的力量，「原來願意發表聲音，真的可以改變歷史。」最後，欣潔說的這段話，很適合作為這段奇幻冒險的總結──「Everything is possible，這麼大的事情都過了，沒有什麼過不去。」是的，我們一起做到了。謝謝大平台，謝謝那段時間一起勇敢的每個人。

初心

DEDICATION

六色彩虹
紅、橙、黃、綠、藍和紫羅蘭色
是同志驕傲旗
是彩虹平權大平台的 LOGO 重要元素
更是一直以來提醒與溫暖我們的精神象徵

雨過天青
是 2019 年 5 月 17 日的天氣變換
是同婚法案通過
也是下一階段挑戰的開始

謹以此書獻給每一位曾經為這場美好改變付出過、一直永保初心的你

在 2019 年 5 月 24 日，擔任台灣第一天同婚登記的紅毯大旗。

The Calm after the Storm:

A PHOTOBOOK OF TAIWAN'S JOURNEY TO MARRIAGE EQUALITY (2016-2019)

- English Version -

PREFACE

The Calm after the Storm

* Please turn to page 32 for Chinese version

There was a period of time where we were always taking to the street for large scale rallies, press conferences, parades, and protests. During these critical moments, it seemed the rain was ever-present, but even the strongest storm could not extinguish the flame of our determination.

December 10, 2016—250,000 people gathered at Ketagalan Boulevard for the Stand Up for Marriage Equality Concert, marking the largest rally since the Sunflower Movement. Over thirty artists joined the cause despite the insufficient budget and minimal organizing experience of the host LGBT rights organizations. Later that night, it poured; yet, multiple artists, perfect makeup and all, still braved the pouring rain to perform and over 100,000 supporters stayed through the storm to the very end.

May 17, 2019—While inside the Legislative Yuan final votes for the same-sex marriage bill were being cast, outside in the pouring rain were supporters who could no longer distinguish between the rain and their own tears as they joyously watched the results for each clause come in. As the banging of the gavel echoed through the chamber hall, confirming the passing of the bill, the sun came out from behind the clouds and a rainbow emerged—a true calm after the storm. The warmth of the sun dried the rain and turned tears into laughter. No one had dared hope they would ever be able to witness this day in Taiwan.

May 24, 2019—Taiwan became the first country in Asia where same-sex couples can get married. To date, over 6,000 same-sex couples have married and gained legal recognition as a family from the government. A number have even gone abroad to access assistive reproductive technologies and now have children. Interpersonal connections and societal structures are like a large organism, and now that same-sex couples are able to legally marry, they can become a part of this organism. This opens the door for many new and diverse narratives and creates further opportunities for change throughout different communities. As for the next generation, they will enjoy a future that is inherently more equitable and diverse. We now sit on the brink of these changes, which may one day be taken for granted; so, through this photobook, the Taiwan Equality Campaign (pre-2020 known as the Marriage Equality Coalition) hopes to set down a record of how what once seemed impossible came to be.

Over the course of the past 30 years, the LGBT rights movement in Taiwan brought many people together who fought for change throughout the many ups and downs of society as a whole and the LGBT community. Though the challenges faced during this time cannot possibly be described in a few words, this book has attempted to offer an inside perspective. We hope that through recording the four years between 2016-2020 in both images in words, we will memorialize the success achieved collaboratively during this unprecedented and unforgettable period of history.

This photobook is dedicated to each and every person who contributed to the marriage equality movement—not only those in Taiwan but also our many supporters abroad, both those currently involved and those who came before us. We would like to take this opportunity to thank everyone who supported and worked for the Marriage Equality Coalition and Taiwan Equality Campaign, past and present. We pushed our physical limits, the limits of our resolve, and the limits of collaboration between individuals and organizations. In return, we learned how to put ourselves aside to work for the greater good, how to work towards a mutual goal, and how to always find a way forward. The journey may have had its difficulties, but it was certainly a lesson we will all always remember.

We know that although there may still be hurdles ahead on the road to equality, we will continue to make progress—together.

Executive Director of the Taiwan Equality Campaign
Jennifer Lu

FOREWORD

A Movement Brought Hope

* Please turn to page 30 for Chinese version

Taiwan's journey to marriage equality, through adversity and uncertainty, provides hope for anyone advocating for human rights for the LGBTIQA+ communities and our families around the world.

The inspiring campaign built public support, pursued legal challenges, defended the community through a public vote, and won the hearts and minds of Taiwan's politicians.

The challenges faced in Taiwan were similar to Australia and the United States of America, two countries who were proud to help support and encourage the amazing activists break new ground and deliver marriage equality to the first country in Asia.

While the day marriage equality became law in Taiwan (24th of May, 2019) was a day of great celebration it followed many emotional and exhausting years of wins and losses sustained by dedicated and determined campaigners and volunteers who can now share their success help future campaigns.

There are many more countries where we must advance the freedom to marry and many more challenges the LGBTIQA+ communities face in Taiwan, Asia, and the rest of the world. The victory of this campaign will help lay the foundation for others and reinforces that we are part of every family, workplace, religion, community and countries and should be treated equally and fairly in all laws.

Personally, I would like to thank Taiwan's marriage equality campaign for working with Australia and advocates around the world. We learnt so much from Taiwan's journey and it continues to inspire us to achieve more here and help others campaigning for fairness and equality around the world.

Chair, Australian Marriage Equality
Member for Sydney, Parliament of NSW
Alex Greenwich

How Love Won in Taiwan

* Please turn to page 31 for Chinese version

Taiwan's Constitutional Court's ruling affirming the freedom to marry in May 2017 kicked off a prolonged battle for LGBT rights – one that traveled from the Judicial Yuan to the ballot box and finally to the Legislative Yuan.

Local advocates worried that the two-year window the ruling gave lawmakers to enact legislation meant that opponents of marriage had time to organize an effort to derail marriage equality entirely.

Leaders like Marriage Equality Coalition Taiwan's Jennifer Lu knew that to make Taiwan the first country in Asia to win marriage, the team would have to build a national campaign to bring the conversation about same-sex couples directly to the Taiwanese people.

Lu's realization mirrored the lessons that we – as veterans and leaders of Freedom to Marry, the campaign that won marriage for same-sex couples in the United States – had learned over decades of struggles. Our work in the US and other countries taught us that the best way to calm our opposition's fear-mongering is to tell the stories of same-sex couples who wanted to marry – showing them alongside the family members, friends, and neighbors who support them – to spark a wider societal conversation.

When the opposition in Taiwan forced marriage equality onto a nationwide referendum, we knew – despite our belief that the dignity of families should never be put to a public vote – that they had inadvertently sparked the largest-scale conversation about LGBT people in Taiwan's history. The referendum offered the opportunity for Taiwanese activists to build a massive campaign rooted in real stories of families. The Marriage Equality Coalition Taiwan would soon become one of the most impressive and large-scale campaigns for the freedom to marry that the world had ever seen.

Marriage Equality Coalition Taiwan enlisted Taiwanese people who spoke from the heart about why they support the LGBT people in their lives. From a 90-year-old grandmother, to a dad who shared his journey towards supporting marriage for his lesbian daughter, to a gay couple who had been together for more than 30 years, these stories were across social media, television, radio, billboards, and the traditional press. These stories signaled to everyday Taiwanese people that not only LGBT people have a stake and a voice in supporting marriage equality. Rather, supporting marriage for same-sex couples is a matter of who they are as Taiwanese people and is an opportunity to live up to and stand up for the values they most hold dear.

In May 2019, Taiwan's LGBT movement delivered Asia's first-ever freedom to marry win – and people celebrated around the world. As the victory continues to sink in, polling showing 60% of Taiwanese people now supporting the freedom to marry offers clear evidence that when you remove the fiery rhetoric and show real couples sharing in marriage, most people understand that same-sex couples marrying doesn't negatively impact their lives.

The enduring impact of Taiwan's monumental win will be felt for years to come – in the power it built for the LGBT movement, in the model it provides for Asia, and in the lives of the loving and committed same-sex couples who can finally stand before their family and friends to say "I do."

Freedom to Marry

Evan Wolfson, Thalia Zepatos, and Cameron Tolle

THE JOURNEY

2016

* Please turn to page 44 for Chinese version

#NOMORE
#standupformarriageequality

"Before love, everyone is equal. My name is Tsai Ing-wen, and I support marriage equality. [I believe] every person should be free to love and pursue happiness." —2016.10.31 Tsai Ying-wen

Continuing the work of Legislator Hsiao Bi-khim whose bill to legalize same-sex marriage was rejected in 2006, Legislators Li-Chiun Cheng and Mei-Nu Yu took up the fight once more in 2014 by jointly introducing a bill to amend marriage civil code. After this bill was shelved, Legislator Mei-Nu Yu and the Marriage Equality Coalition, hoping to realize marriage equality, once again introduced a bill to amend civil code in 2016 .

But on December 3, 2016, a group of protestors against LGBT rights held a mass rally on Ketagalan Boulevard. Their campaign of misinformation incited the LGBT community to push back. Hoping to boost morale, the Marriage Equality Coalition called for an emergency mobilization of supporters and took to the streets to show them the LGBT community would not be defeated. It was in this way that the No More—Stand Up for Marriage Equality concert came to be, attracting 250,000 supporters to Ketagalan Boulevard on December 10, Human Rights Day. This display of support marked a high point in the 30 years of the LGBT rights movement in Taiwan.

Things had been building to this moment for some time. In 2012, Tsai Ing-wen, chair of the Democratic Progressive Party (DPP) at the time, expressed support for three bills proposed by the Taiwan Alliance to Promote Civil Partnership Rights (TAPCPR). These bills were largely modelled on French legislation which was approved by parliament in 2013 and legalized gay marriage and adoption for same-sex couples. But while the larger landscape continued to change, Taiwan still had a long way to go; that same year, several media outlets reported how many people were alarmed by the portion of Taiwan's mandated gender equity education that teaches about the LGBT community. The media storm caused a great blow to gender equity education in schools.

Then, after the 2014 bill to legalize same-sex marriage was shelved following the first reading, alternatives to marriage began to emerge. The Kaohsiung City, Taipei City, and Taichung City municipal governments began allowing same-sex couples to register as a household in 2015. While this granted registered couples the right to make medical decisions for their partners, the national law had still not been amended; as a result, it was up to the hospital whether or not they would allow same-sex partners to make these decisions.

But things began to look up in 2015. Chi Chia-wei, who had unsuccessfully petitioned the Taipei District Court to marry his male partner in 1986, once again went to the courts to petition a review of his case. At the same time, three lesbian couples attempted to file for marriage at the Taipei City Household Registration Office, and in response, the Taipei City government requested a constitutional interpretation from the Supreme Court.

Attention turned once again to the lack of legal protections of same-sex couples when, on October 16, 2016, Professor Jacques Picoux, who had shared a home for 35 years with his loving partner, Tseng Ching-chao, fell to his death from a ten-story building. The pride parade was held on the following day and over 80,000 people marched.

By November 2016, the Legislative Yuan had passed the first reading of a bill to amend civil code to allow same-sex marriage. However, opponents of marriage equality aggressively pushed back. Many groups, all of whom allude to defending families in their organization name, issued emotional appeals to "Protect the Family Unit." In addition to aggressively disseminationg homophobic propaganda, they made many hurtful statements about the LGBT community at public hearings on the issue of marriage equality. Legislator Hsieh Chi-ta Chou, for one, stated that "Gay people are cockroaches. They'll multiply." Even the head of the Law Department at Shih Hsin University, Yu-zong Wu, made a discriminatory statement insinuating that allowing LGBT couples to adopt would be like permitting "the Nazis to conduct human experiments."

Despite the barbaric treatment, the LGBT community rallied. There were frequent calls to mobilize throughout November and December. The call would be issued through Facebook event pages, and once it was sent, many would take off work just to attend. On December 10, 2016, the Marriage Equality Coalition organized the No More Stand Up for Marriage Equality concert on Ketagalan Boulevard. Not only did 250,000 people attend, a reflection of growing public support for marriage equality, but over 30 artists and bands eagerly volunteered to perform pro bono. That night the names of all of those who had once fallen victim to societal expectations of gender temperament and sexuality, such as Yeh Yung-Chih, Lin Qinghui and Shi Jiya, and Jacques Picoux, were projected onto the brick facade of the presidential office in memoriam. As the crowd looked up at the names, they shed tears for the loss of life.

That year, the LGBT community was carried through by the strength of the community. The community refused to be demoralized by others saying the LGBT community would multiply like cockroaches. Instead, they remembered the words of Deserts Chang at the public hearing when she quoted the words

of the U.S. Supreme Court: "The Constitution cannot control such prejudices but neither can it tolerate them" and that of Jay Lin, the CEO of Portico Media, who once said, "What we want is simple: we want legal protection for our lives with our partners and children."

2017

* Please turn to page 62 for Chinese version

#AsiasBeaconofEquality
#MarriageEqualityVStheLY

In February, four groups from the Marriage Equality Coalition accepted an invitation to the Presidential Office for talks with the president in anticipation of the upcoming constitutional interpretation. Leading up to the interpretation, much of the focus of the Marriage Equality Coalition was on education campaigns to increase acceptance of the LGBT community and reduce social division among the middle-aged and older demographics. Similar to the methods of U.S. rights groups during their fight for marriage equality, experts from the fields of psychology, law, social work, education, politics, gender studies, and public health had been recruited to strengthen the LGBT rights movement's argument for full marriage equality. Their voices contributed to Facebook campaigns initiated by the Marriage Equality Coalition such as Missing: LGBT Rights and Letters to the Grand Justices: Tell Your Story.

Once the momentous day, May 24, finally arrived, the Marriage Equality Coalition mobilized marriage equality supporters to rally outside of the Legislative Yuan. Everyone was nervous as they gathered together, it was unknown whether or not the interpretation would support same-sex marriage, but still rainbow flags flew throughout the crowd. While there were people handing out flyers and dressed strikingly, the atmosphere of camaraderie that day was different from the joy typically shared during something like a pride parade. At this point, there was no turning back; everyone held their breath.

Evening fell and it began to rain; yet, the crowd continued to grow. Finally, the Judicial Yuan's Secretary-General emerged to read the decision: "The authorities concerned shall amend or enact relevant laws, in accordance with the ruling of this Interpretation, within two years from the issuance of this interpretation. It is within the discretion of the authorities concerned to determine the formality for achieving the equal protection of the freedom of marriage." As the announcement echoed through the crowd, the rain subsided and a rainbow emerged. Those who had persevered through the LGBT rights movement wept freely. Taking the stage, Hsiao Bi-khim declared, "Everyone is worthy of love. Everyone deserves happiness. The rainbow above us, shines over Taiwan, shines over the world, shines over human rights."

After the grand justices issued Judicial Yuan Interpretation No. 748 ordering that same-sex couples should have "equal protection of their rights and freedom to marry," not only did the LGBT rights movement become a model for other social movements, but Taiwan also became a beacon of hope for the LGBT community in Asia. Following in Taiwan's footsteps, various LGBT rights movements in Asia have grown stronger over the years. In Japan, for instance, several LGBT couples have sued the government for discrimination. And in South Korea, the annual pride parade has continued to attract more supporters.

However, while many people were quick to congratulate the Taiwanese LGBT community for their success, those involved in the LGBT rights movement knew the fight for marriage equality was far from over. They continued to nurse their old wounds while continuing the fight to gain more supporters.
In the months following the interpretation, the Marriage Equality Coalition closely followed legislative developments and public sentiment. At the same time, they expanded their campaign to raise public awareness about the LGBT community and restructured their online and offline strategies in order to benefit the most people possible. Online, fact-checking and correcting misinformation spread by anti-LGBT rights groups took priority. Offline, the Marriage Equality Coalition participated in a large number of events internationally. In light of the interpretation, the Marriage Equality Coalition was invited to human rights events hosted by the United Nations, to Washington D.C., to the Human Rights Campaign (the largest LGBT organization in the U.S.), and to present to the Taiwanese community in the U.S.. Jennifer Lu, the Marriage Equality Coalition's executive director at the time, accepted interviews from many countries and many time zones, speaking out in cities all over the world in hopes of raising awareness for the marriage equality movement in Taiwan.

This international attention helped to improve the morale of the LGBT rights movement, and pride parades all over the country saw greater numbers of supporters. Realizing the importance of communicating with those outside of one's own social circle, the Marriage Equality Coalition began strategically targeting more rural areas and using Taiwanese during their dialogues with the communities there. As a result, a greater number of local politicians became more aware of the movement. And the Marriage Equality Coalition didn't just communicate with people, but also with the divine. They joined the Dajia pilgrimage for Goddess Matsu and asked for her blessings.

There were times during 2017 where it seemed as though the bill would never break free of the quagmire of social resistance and legal barriers, yet determined LGBT rights advocates never gave up and continued to press on.

2018

* Please turn to page 82 for Chinese version

#fightforlovevote2yes3no
#gohomeandvote
#waitingonabetterfuture
#moveforwardtogether

On October 9, 2018, the Central Election Commission announced petition signatures for referendum proposals 10, 11, and 12 initiated by the Coalition for the Happiness of Our Next Generation and proposals 14 and 15 initiated by Miao Poya passed the legal threshold of petitions needed and would be included on the November referendum ballot.

Vote Yes on:

Question 14: Do you agree that the rights of same-sex couples getting married should be regulated under civil code?

Question 15: Do you agree that all levels of education should include curriculum on the importance of gender equality, affective education, sex education, and LGBT issues in accordance with the guidelines of the Gender Equality Education Act?

Vote No on:

Question 10: Do you agree that marriage as defined by the Civil Code should be restricted to a union between one man and one woman?

Question 11: Do you agree that the Ministry of Education should not implement the Enforcement Rules of the Gender Equality Education Act in elementary and middle schools?

Question 12: Do you agree that civil code should not be changed and another method should be implemented to protect the rights of same-sex couples who have agreed to permanantly live together?

This was the year of urging others to vote yes on 14 &15 and no on 10, 11, 12 in the November referendums. It was also a time where many LGBT individuals decided to come out to their families and discuss with family members how they planned to cast their vote. Though there was a fair amount of disagreement, there were many compromises as well.

Looking for campaign strategies, the Marriage Equality Coalition learned from those who had been through referendums in the past. At the beginning of 2018, they travelled to Ireland and invited experienced groups to Taiwan from Australia and the U.S. to share their campaign methods.

Locally, the Marriage Equality Coalition implemented community outreach initiatives: engaging in discussions, setting up booths in traditional markets and shopping centers, and training group leaders. On the streets, volunteers took on the taxing job of talking to voters outside subway stations where they were often confronted by the opposing faction. Then there were the many press conferences, seminars on equal rights, and exhibits where the Marriage Equality Coalition wove in the life stories of LGBT individuals and corrected misinformation about Taiwan's gender equity education, the LGBT community, and LGBT rights. After all, a greater awareness of the LGBT community would mean more people who recognized LGBT individuals as people too. Finally, for the LGBT community members themselves, the Marriage Equality Coalition hosted classes on emotional and mental well-being as the referendum edged nearer.

The 2018 referendums were particularly unique because they were the first to be held after major changes to the law lowered requirements to get a referendum on the ballot. As a result, there were many different issues to vote on making this not only a confusing time for the gender equality movement but for voters as well.

During this tumultuous time, the Marriage Equality Coalition and anti-LGBT groups such as the Coalition for the Happiness of our Next Generation clashed via press statements. Misinformation and fake news shared over social media was a particular problem, and many chose to leave family group chats after disagreements. Volunteers for the Marriage Equality Coalition increased the breadth of the campaign operations—venturing outside of Taipei to host talks and forums. In addition, more resources were deployed to organizations centered in rural areas where volunteers passed out flyers, initiated dialogues, and faced a lot of pushback. One strikingly emotional campaign from that year featured individuals speaking to important family members they had lost in order to encourage LGBT individuals to communicate openly with those who are most important to them. And before the referendum, the Go Home and Vote for Love concert attracted an audience of 100,000 people, solidifying the determination of the community.

The day before the referendum, November 23, volunteers made a final push to sway the vote, stationing themselves at train stations all over the island holding up signs that read "Welcome Home Voters! National Transport Service." [Translator's Note: Taiwan requires voters to return to the polling center assigned to where their huji is registered. For many, this may be in a different location than where they live.]

However, despite the relentless efforts of LGBT rights advocates, the results of the referendum were devastating.

In light of this defeat, many focused their concerns on the mental health of the LGBT community. Lectures helped to encourage community members, reminding them that everyone would continue to move forward together. And while too many tears were shed that year, what was surprising was that even the referendum results were unable to discourage LGBT rights supporters. It wasn't only them who persisted; the stories of those whose lives

had been changed by advocacy work impacted others as well.

One such example was 93 year-old Chun Tao. In an campaign advertisement supporting same-sex marriage, she affectionately voiced her support for her 37 year-old granddaughter, Xiao Rou, to be able to marry her girlfriend. "I want to give a toast at their wedding," she says in the ad, her loving smile lighting up billboards across the country.

There was also Ho (75) and Wang (57) who shared their story in articles published in newspapers and magazines: they had already grown old together, their relationship was solid, they just lacked a marriage certificate.

It turns out that love is unbreakable.

Even though the Marriage Equality Coalition may have been unable to alter the opinions of the anti-LGBT faction, the referendum results weren't all disappointing. A year of intense grassroots activism, relentless digital and printed advertisements, and an awareness campaign ultimately resulted in three million votes in support of marriage rights.

Following the referendum, the Marriage Equality Coalition decided to refocus their efforts on lobbying the Legislative Yuan. Opposition groups had released a barrage of misinformation during their referendum campaign, and the Marriage Equality Coalition was determined not to let it get in the way of marriage equality. At this point, separate legislation legalizing same-sex marriage was the only way forward, and so the goal became to ensure that same-sex marriage rights were in no way inferior to those accorded to heterosexual couples.

The year ended with the community drying their tears, picking each other back up, and reorganizing once more. This had been an unfair battle against an adversary with far greater resources. Ahead was a long fight, but having gotten this far, the only option was forward.

2019

* Please turn to page 106 for Chinese version

#nocompromise
#can'tlosethevote
#notoneless
#startofhappiness
#gaymarriagestartsNOW

The direction of the Marriage Equality Coalition's 2019 agenda was clear in light of the 2018 referendum results. Though society as a whole seemed to be accepting of the LGBT community, but this simply wasn't a match for the deep pockets of the anti-LGBT rights organizations. So as the LGBT community saw many of its members struggle with self-harm and even loss of life, efforts turned to comforting the community and consulting experts for help. Still, the community had to brush away their tears and continue lobbying efforts to find a solution that would allow marriage equality without amending the civil code.

Under pressure from multiple parties, Premier Su Tseng-chang of the Executive Yuan introduced a draft resolution to legalize same-sex marriage on February 22. This display of commitment to protecting the rights of the LGBT community was titled the Act for Implementation of Judicial Yuan Interpretation No. 748. Needing the support of policy makers, the Marriage Equality Coalition scheduled many appointments and phone calls. They also mobilized supporters to comment on the Facebook pages of legislators in order to inform them about the real will of the people.

Flash mobs, press conferences, social media campaigns, estimating vote numbers, the LGBT rights movement did everything possible, but it never felt like enough. Everyone in the community found this period of time exciting but also terrifying. Would the community be hurt once more? It felt like a race against time.

May 17 finally arrived; it was the day the

Legislative Yuan would vote on the same-sex marriage bill. It was pouring outside of the Legislative Yuan where supporters were gathered, a determined look in their eyes as they shouted, "The Vote Must Pass!" They hoped, for both the LGBT community as a whole and the sake of everyone affected, that they could get through this. Anxious, nervous, distressed, and hopeful, the crowd held their breath as vote results for each clause of the bill were projected on stage. And as the light after light lit up, indicating a vote in support, the crowd didn't dare believe their eyes. What they had worked for was finally coming true. Tears streamed down their faces as they embraced. The bill actually passed. It was real. Same-sex marriage was finally legal.

The weather finally cleared up at the end of the vote. Though cliche, it felt as though the weather was a reflection of the crowd's emotional state. This was a day for the LGBT community to celebrate! More than 50,000 people stood in front of the Legislative Yuan; they had trodden a rough path and certainly weren't afraid of a little rain. It was important that, together, they bore witness to this historical moment—the passage of the bill legalizing same-sex marriage. As for the many couples who had lived together in committed relationships for many years, but were missing a key piece of paper, they could finally get their marriage certificate. The bill had passed.

LGBT couples returned home, and life returned to normal: couples cooked, cleaned, fought, and made up, but their relationships felt acknowledged, sanctioned, and closer than before. Finally, they could tell their friends and family to save the date.

The sun shined brightly on May 24, the first day same-sex marriage went into effect. It was truly a good day to get married. The Marriage Equality Coalition organized mass weddings in Taipei and Kaohsiung and, together with the Taipei City Civil Affairs Bureau, hosted a reception for a number of same-sex couples. Well-known couples like

Chen Xue and Zaocanren registered to be married after ten years together as did Li-Ying Chien and her partner who goes by the pen name Cynical Chick. In total, over 500 same-sex couples received their new ID that day, the spouse column on the back finally filled in—a seemingly minor change but representative of hard-earned recognition.

2020 & 2021

* Please turn to page 138 for Chinese version

In 2020, the Marriage Equality Coalition formally changed its name to the Taiwan Equality Campaign, and their 2019 focus on campaigning and lobbying shifted to a focus on community education, open dialogue, and international collaboration. While the 2018 referendums made it clear that a person's beliefs cannot change overnight, the Taiwan Equality Campaign set out to raise awareness for all ends of the spectrum in all corners of society.

To this end, the Taiwan Equality Campaign continued to demand further legislation to ensure equal rights such as that to allow same-sex couples to adopt as a couple. They also assisted 15 gay couples in the surrogacy process, facilitated three dialogues about the rights of transnational couples, and participated in 33 negotiations. By the end of 2020, they had successfully lobbied 20 legislators to support the draft for the adoption law, allowing it to pass the first reading.

By this point, same-sex couples could legally get married, but for many this meant coming out if they were to have a wedding reception or apply for marriage leave from work. It became clear that workplace discrimination needed to be addressed through more dialogues and education work. Between 2020 and 2021, the newly-named Taiwan Equality Campaign

closely followed LGBT public sentiment. A survey they conducted revealed that in all environments—such as the work place or school campuses—there was still a ways to go to reach equality. So even after same-sex marriage was legalized, the calls for the LGBT community to take to the streets continued; but this time, rather, it was not to change the opinions of others but to broaden the community's own understanding of circles outside their own.

With the outbreak of Covid-19, the Taiwan Equality Campaign had to find ways to continue their public education campaigns. The decision was made to leverage digital platforms in order to hold casual discussions on topics concerning the LGBT individual, the workplace, and society at large. Jennifer Lu started the YouTube channel "Time to Come Out," shot videos like "Should sexuality stay out of politics?," and appeared in a video hosted by Sebastian Lin "I'm sensitive, okay? Now about the workplace...". During this time, podcasts in Taiwan really took off and offered an approachable, realistic format to interact with netizens. So, the Taiwan Equality Campaign began the podcast "Girl, let me tell you…" where relationship veterans talked about everything from breakups and intimate relationships to mental and physical health. In comparison with the campaigns led for the referendum and marriage equality, this work was far more nuanced and sustainable.

And though the past few years have been long and arduous, the Taiwan Equality Campaign knows they will see progress with a bit more patience and attention. This is why they continue to work with both the government and public to achieve ends such as improving the same-sex marriage bill so it encompasses all the same rights accorded to heterosexual couples including benefits in new legislation aimed at boosting the birth rate. Demands such as these are always seen through to the very end, advocating for equality down to the finest detail, such as the use of neutral language in government paperwork rather than "Mother and Father" or "Husband and Wife."

This work has helped Taiwan to celebrate several firsts in 2021. In April, a member of Taiwan's intelligence and national security force, Aris Tsai, married her partner; despite being a traditionally conservative branch of the government, the Minister of Justice, Ching-hsiang Tsai, and three former Investigation Bureau Director Generals were all in attendance. Shortly after, in May, Ting Tse-yan and Guzifer Leong obtained an important victory for transnational same-sex couples. They had won a case allowing the Macau-Taiwanese couple to get married. [Translator's note: At time of publication, Taiwanese law governing the marriage of transnational couples varied depending on the nationality of the foreign partner.]

Around the same time, pictures circulated of music producer Isaac Chen and his partner welcoming a new baby boy into the world. While the community was happy for them, they had not forgotten the many LGBT families who were still waiting for the legalization of all transnational marriages, equal adoption laws, and equal access to assistive reproductive technologies—all important issues in the past two years of the LGBT rights movement.

After events originally planned to celebrate the first anniversary of same-sex marriage were cancelled due to Covid-19, the Taiwan Equality Campaign was determined to do something for the second anniversary. To boost the spirits of the community, they hosted the online event "Follow the Rainbow: Join in the Fun." The Taiwan Equality Campaign also came out with a rainbow iPass card as a little way for people to show their support and love of the LGBT community.

And though the Covid-19 epidemic may be far from over, the Taiwan Equality Campaign continues in its work to influence policy and lobby politicians so that one day same-sex couples can enjoy all the rights accorded to heterosexual couples. One day, marriage rights will not be limited by nationality. Marriage restrictions preventing certain transnational marriages will be removed. One day, family rights will be equal. The same-sex marriage law will be amended so that couples can jointly adopt a child. One day, access to assistive reproductive technologies will be equal. Same-sex couples will not have to travel great lengths to places like the U.S. or Canada because they will have access at home. However, laws must be amended first so that the pride flag can fly freely across all of Taiwan.

The Taiwan Equality Campaign continues to light the way so that those in the LGBT community, those who once took to the streets for equal rights, can one day enjoy better, more comprehensive rights and protections.

Overhead, the pride flag continues, and will continue, to fly proudly.

AN ONGOING PURSUIT OF GREATER EQUALITY

Mei-Nu Yu & Yu-Jen Hsu

* Please turn to page 142 for Chinese version

· Mei-Nu Yu (Lawyer; Former Democratic Progressive Party Legislator)
· Yu-Jen Hsu (Monte Jade Science & Technology Association of Taiwan Chief Secretary; Former Kuomintang Party Legislator)

Between 2016-2020 Mei-Nu Yu and Yu-Jen Hsu were both serving in the Legislative Yuan, and their offices were on the same floor. The two legislators often ran into each other in the elevator and developed a routine banter.

"How's the Kuomintang party (KMT) doing?" Yu would ask.

"I wouldn't know," Hsu would reply before returning the question, "What about the Democratic Progressive Party (DPP)?"

In turn, Yu would tell him, "I wouldn't know either."

This simple exchange was a reflection of just how marginalized the two legislators had become within their respective political parties as a result of advocating for the legalization of same-sex marriage.

It was May 2019, and the Legislative Yuan was soon to vote on the finalized Act for Implementation of Judicial Yuan Interpretation No. 748, the legislation detailing the new same-sex marriage law. Leading up to this vote, the DPP decided to keep Yu out of all related negotiations. She explained, "They said everyone already knew what I was going to say. I suppose they were worried I would get into a confrontation with the opposing legislators." For a period of time, she would be frequently pulled aside by fellow DPP legislators who would complain, "Mei-Nu, I'm going to lose my district because of you."

Hsu didn't have things much better. He was a newcomer to politics who was constantly being told by senior colleagues to keep his head down, vote with the party, and remain quiet. The day before the vote, he received a concerned phone call.

"I was told not to speak [before the voting procedures], but I took my turn at the rostrum anyways. After returning to my seat, the legislator next to me turned to me and said, 'Didn't I tell you not to make a speech?' Later that day, I watched him get incrementally madder as I voted yes for each individual clause in the bill." As he recalled the experience, Hsu mischievously added a quick online search will tell you just which legislator it was.

For Human Rights: 30 Years Against the Current

Both Yu and Hsu had to steel themselves against public opposition to support same-sex marriage, the former having been well prepared to do so by her background in the women's rights movement. In the 1980's, Yu joined the Awakening Foundation, a Taiwanese NPO dedicated to fighting for gender equality and women's empowerment. "I really started to find my confidence after joining the women's rights movement and no longer cared about what people thought of me," said Yu. "I cared about doing the right thing and about being responsible for my own actions."

During this time, Yu was instrumental in amending

the Act of Gender Equality in Employment and revising civil code to ensure greater equality around the decision of whether a child will take the surname of their mother or father.
Yu was elected to the Legislative Yuan in 2012 and soon demonstrated that the thornier the issue, the more she wanted to take it on. Despite significant opposition, during her time in office, Yu was successful in passing the Family Act, decriminalizing adultery, and amending civil code to ensure greater equality of property ownership between married couples.

It was also in 2012 when Yu first proposed amending the civil code to legalize same-sex marriage. Over the seven years that followed, up until 2019 when the new legislation allowing same-sex marriage finally passed, Yu said she never considered giving up.

"I worked for the women's rights movement for thirty years. It always took around 10 years for any piece of women's rights legislation to come to fruition. Typically, it took a tragedy, someone getting hurt or dieing, before the law would pass." Yu cited the civil code regulating child surnames as an example; Yu pushed for several years before civil code was amended in 2007 requiring parents to agree in writing if the child would assume the father's surname or the mother's surname. It wasn't until 2010 that it was amended once more allowing for legal adults to be able to change their surname on their own.

Yu reflected, "We were condemned for merely wanting to allow surname changes. It was all over the news. Newspapers were publishing critical pieces by reporters, anthropologists, and scholars. Yet, two years later in 2010, when we wanted to amend the law once more to allow legal adults to be able to change their own surname, the public was totally indifferent."

It's always the first step towards change that is the most terrifying. Yu, in particular, has become very familiar with this type of backlash

in the face of big structural changes and, as a result, has built up tremendous courage to work for what's right, despite the headwinds.

Unfettered

Hsu, on the other hand, had zero background in neither politics nor social activism. While he was serving on a youth advisory committee to the Executive Yuan, he fortuitously fell into the good graces of the former premier C.K. Mao, which may be why he was selected to be on the coveted electoral list of KMT Legislative Yuan candidates. By being on the electoral list, Hsu did not have to run for a district seat; instead, if the KMT party received a sufficient proportion of votes, he would be allocated a seat. When he agreed to the nomination, he assumed he would merely be riding on the coattails of the stronger candidates. So he was shocked upon hearing that he would be fifth to be allocated a seat, a top spot, and was essentially guaranteed to win.

Most were shocked by this development. Even Yu was taken aback and began to question her own judgement. She laughed, "We had met before he was elected. My thought was that he should've been nominated by the DPP, not the KMT! I was dumbfounded."

Hsu simply laughed and said that the DPP did not approach him. "I really didn't have any political leanings anyways," Hsu explained. "I thought maybe I could mix things up a little in a conservative party like the KMT by providing a new perspective. Maybe I could even serve as a bridge between the two parties. That's why I was willing to run." But just why did he decide to advocate for same-sex marriage?

The 2016 election coincided with Taiwan's marriage equality movement. Coming from the diverse, liberal startup world, it was a given that Hsu would support LGBT rights, but it was a business trip with a colleague that initially led him to have a more subtle understanding of the challenges faced by the LGBT community. "My colleague and I were on the plane when she told me she was gay and that she didn't dare tell her family. She was really struggling and didn't know how to cope with others treating her differently. It made a really big impact on me." Hsu reasoned, "There are only 100 legislators, but we have the power to change history. After being elected, I decided that I would push for that change."

Despite knowing he would face challenges, he said, "I wanted to act. I wanted everyone to look back on what I accomplished." I Isu's foray into the world of politics was a bit of a fluke afterall, so he didn't have much to lose. Maybe, just maybe, he could use his four year term to further his own ideals towards a better Taiwan .

He first created a stir during the Legislative Yuan's regular morning session by saying he wanted "Taiwan to become the first country in Asia with legalized same-sex marriage." He then went on to suggest the KMT propose amending the law to allow for same-sex marriage

At the time, Yu was in charge of the Judiciary and Organic Laws and Statutes Committee (JOLSC), a committee whose responsibilities include deliberating government organization, systems, and rules. This meant that Yu had the authority to schedule when legislation would be deliberated. But as a part of the majority party, she also had to consider the big picture and so, at times, was not quite as free to do what she pleased as Hsu was. Hsu said, "Legislator Yu and I had an unstated agreement that allowed us to use our positions as members of the majority and minority parties in a complementary way."

Isolated within his own party for his stance, Hsu decided to push things to the limit, "I decided to propose we reform the law to the most progressive degree possible: a direct amendment of the current civil code rather than a separate law. I chose to launch the offensive." This strategy was aimed at putting pressure on the majority party, after all, how would it look if the minority party that opposed same-sex marriage proposed legislation that was more progressive than the supporting majority party?

Acting Individually, Advancing Collectively

The more influential members of the KMT, however, did not take Hsu's suggestion seriously; yet, this may have worked in his favor. "I brought in a proposal to gather signatures from my colleagues, and they signed it," said Hsu. He laughed, "Maybe they just assumed it would never be scheduled, and I was just being naive. But I got lucky, ten or so legislators signed on, including senior legislators such as Jin-Pyng Wang. It may be that they didn't know what they had signed."

As a result, this improbable proposal became one of three to move to committee, the other two proposals being raised by Yu and the New Power Party. On the fateful day of committee deliberation, November 17, 2016, Yu sat at the head of the JOLSC. The KMT legislators demanded thirty public hearings before continuing the deliberation process. When this suggestion met opposition, a scuffle began at the front of the chamber.

Yu reflected on the tumultuous day, "I immediately contacted several LGBT organizations. Everyone was insistent that we could not support holding even a single public hearing. We had listened to the same arguments on repeat for years; we knew what would be said. However, the KMT wouldn't back down, and it quickly became a battle."

When it reached four p.m. and the two parties had still not reached a deal, the head of the Legislative Yuan General Affairs Section urged Yu to adjourn for the day telling her, "If you don't call to adjourn, you're putting our lives in danger." By then, protesters were lined up outside and ready to burst into the Legislative Yuan. But the negotiations were not yet complete. Yu and the DPP had convinced KMT legislators to reduce the number of required public hearings from thirty to two, but the KMT was still unwilling to sign off. It wasn't until the KMT saw the session was about to be adjourned that they finally signed at the last minute. Yu recounted, "The moment they finished signing. Someone posing as a reporter charged into the chamber and was restrained by the bailiff. We could hear all the shouting outside. It was really stressful."

Though she initially wasn't sure why the KMT decided to sign, it was because of this that the legislation was able to move forward. Afterwards their reasons came more into focus, Yu revealed, "I found out that the LGBT organizations I had talked to mobilized all of their contacts in order to call key KMT supporters. These key supporters then lobbied the leaders of the KMT and urged them to compromise. I'm very grateful I had the support of these organizations."

Deliberations were scheduled to continue after the two public hearings; these hearings were held several days later on November 24 and 28 and hosted by the two convenors of the JOLSC, Mei-Nu Yu (DPP) and Shu-Hua Hsu (KMT). By December 26, 2016, the three proposals had been successfully revised to be combined into two different versions, one calling for amending the civil code and the other for creating new legislation. These two proposals were then finally formally sent forward to the next stage in the legislative process. Despite the initial conflicts, Yu expressed she feels the peaceful consensus they ultimately reached was a sign of a mature democracy.

As for Hsu, that day was a real eye-opener for him as a newcomer who had only seen legislators get into physical fights on television. "That day was very, very stressful," he said. "The two parties clashed from the very start. I think it all started when Legislator Sra Kacaw (KMT) charged up to the podium and ripped out the microphone." Seeing his colleague take the lead, Hsu wasn't sure what was expected of him as a KMT member. "It was very awkward. I wasn't sure if I should join the commotion in the front or not." Unfortunately, there was no handbook given to new legislators explaining the expectations, but the consequences of

not meeting these expectations soon became clear. When Hsu did not support the motion to host public hearings, the looks his colleagues shot at him immediately let him know that "the road ahead would be full of hardship and resistance."

Loss and Consolation

Parallel to the progress in the Legislative Yuan, on May 24, 2017, the grand justices of the constitutional court issued Constitutional Interpretation No. 748, officially ruling existing civil code, which did not allow two persons of the same sex to be legally married, violated the Constitution's guarantees of freedom of marriage. The ruling set a two year deadline to amend the law, and if the legal provisions allowing same-sex couples to get married were not enacted within that time, then same-sex couples could legally get married under existing civil code.

Following the interpretation, groups pushing for marriage equality became more active than ever, but so did opposing conservative groups who locked onto the 2018 elections as their last opportunity to be heard. The conservative groups began to mobilize their resources and organize a petition for a referendum opposing amending civil code to allow same-sex marriage. Not to be outdone, the marriage equality groups also petitioned their own referendum but ended up suffering a huge defeat.

In 2021, now officially retired, Yu has the same signature look as she did during her time in office: a fuschia suit jacket and streaks of bright red in her hair. Thinking back on the referendum results from 2018, she vividly recalled, "I felt really down after the referendum. It was very frustrating. Many in the LGBT community at the time were considering giving up. But, personally, I felt that we had already gotten this far, and the DPP was still in control of both the executive and legislative branches. Our core values of freedom, democracy, rule of law, and human rights had not changed; there was no reason to stop just

because of the referendum setback."
A lawyer by profession, Yu was disappointed but still able to see things rationally—the fight was not yet lost. She explained, "The loss of the 2018 referendum only meant that we could not amend the civil code, but we could still create separate legislation. My concern was the degree of protection this new legislation would offer. The constitutional court had clearly stated that it must protect same-sex couple's free and equal right to marriage, but I wasn't certain the new legislation would necessarily meet these constitutional requirements."

Hsu added, "It was really too bad that same-sex marriage became a wedge issue in the 2018 election. It became something all candidates manipulated in order to mobilize voters." Even more daunting, after the referendum was defeated, public opposition to same-sex marriage grew stronger. For Hsu, this meant he "was under a lot of pressure because the KMT swept the midterm elections in 2018, and conservative voices within the party were on the rise." After realizing that they were able to win their elections because of their conservative stance, the KMT wanted this momentum to continue in order to win the 2020 presidential election. To them, Hsu was getting in their way.

Over in the DPP camp, Yu also felt very isolated. Majority Speaker Chien-Ming Ker said to the media, "Mei-Nu Yu, please, don't do this to the DPP." Yu thought long and hard about how to respond. The next morning, it suddenly came to her: "I asked my aides to do some research and found that the number of LGBT individuals that had reported bullying or died by suicide had increased after the referendum. I responded to Ker by sharing these statistics with the media." This response not only defused tensions within the DPP but also gave new strength to many in the LGBT community to keep going.

In response, the LGBT community encouraged her as well. "I was very, very touched," said Yu. "People I didn't even know from the

LGBT community, and even some who were not LGBT, bravely spoke out. They called or sent cards to reassure me and thank me for my work. It was very sweet. People my age tend to keep their emotions to themselves, but I realized just how different the younger generation is in this regard. My office now has an entire wall that is full of these cards."

Hsu also has a wall of thank you notes and letters of encouragement. Though it has been three years since the 2018 referendums, he clearly remembers the dismay he felt as the results were announced. However, this dismay did not last for long. "After we mourned," he said, "we came back determined and took action. We showed that together we can overcome being misunderstood and even hostility."

The Rainbow After the Storm

It was May 23, 2019, the day before voting for the final legislation to implement same-sex marriage (Act for Implementation of J.Y. Interpretation No. 748). Premier Su Tseng-chang convened all of the DPP legislators where, according to Yu, he made a moving appeal. "Premier Su spoke about the origins of the DPP and the life-threatening danger and risk founding members bore at the party's inception. Premier Su said, 'In comparison, the risk of losing a few votes is miniscule. There is nothing to fear. One day in the future your grandchildren will ask why you didn't vote for this bill. What will you tell them? This is the direction in which the world is moving; we should stand on the right side of history.'" This earnest speech, Yu believes, played a critical role in the voting results.

Premier Su also posted publicly on Facebook urging all DPP legislators to vote in support of the bill. Hsu was concerned by this: "I was worried that the issue would once again become a standoff between political parties. There was a legislator in our messaging group that suggested that since the DPP called for a party-line vote, the KMT should too. They claimed this would show their party was united and that there can be no in between." In response, the next day during the KMT's morning caucus, Hsu tried to remind everyone of the values at stake. "I said the DPP has turned this vote into a party issue but we shouldn't. We should show everyone our votes are based on our values."

As Yu and Hsu stepped into the Legislative Yuan on May 24, 2019, they were both concerned the bill wouldn't have enough votes to pass. The two legislators intently watched the board of legislator names at the front of the chamber which would light up in green for a vote in support or red for a vote against. Clause after clause, the green lights slowly erased their concern, with little remaining after the key fourth and seventh clauses passed. Yu was ecstatic. DPP colleague Mark Chih Wei Ho excitedly ran over to show Yu his phone and said, "Legislator Yu, look at the comments. Everyone's saying you're like the Goddess Matsu, a saint, a savior."

Watching the green lights, Hsu's career over the past four years flashed before his eyes. "This is what serving as a legislator feels like," he thought. He realized he had helped accomplish something amazing.

The rain outside the Legislative Yuan subsided, and a rainbow emerged over the cheering crowd as many embraced in relief, all because Mei-Nu Yu and Yu-Jen Hsu stood by their values. Though they were of different political parties, used different methods, and faced many with different opinions, together they helped to begin a new chapter in Taiwan's history. As a result, they were able to bring immeasurable happiness to many.

....

Q & A

What does normal mean?

Hsu: The question of whether something is normal or not is an oversimplification. It's very divisive. When we label something as normal, it means, by default, there is something that is not normal, so I don't like to think of things in this way.

Yu: "Normal" is typically determined by the majority, influential individuals, or rulers. Whatever is mainstream is considered normal while what isn't mainstream is abnormal. When we talk about gender mainstreaming, we are talking about how to pull those who have been marginalized into the mainstream. Once they have been brought into the mainstream, we then focus on doing the same for those who are even further marginalized.

What is love?

Hsu: Love is empathizing with those around you. It's important to ask yourself, are you able to love others as you love yourself?

Yu: The most important part of love is that it is unconditional. Many people will talk about what someone must do or cannot do in order for them to love someone else. But how can true love be conditional?

....

Huai-Jen Lee

* Please turn to page 152 for Chinese version

· Huai-Jen Lee (iPass Board Chair; Former Advisor to Su Tseng-chang)

In the corner of the Executive Yuan sat a man who was repeatedly crossing out and revising his notes as he assessed: Whose vote was secure? Whose vote would possibly switch? And who was absolutely unable to be persuaded?

There was only two weeks until the vote on the Act for Implementation of Judicial Yuan Interpretation No. 748, the same-sex marriage bill, and senior political advisor Huai-Jen Lee was restless as he mulled over if there were any other connections that he could use to secure votes and whether or not the senior party members made the calls they had promised to make.

Thinking back on that period of time, Lee said, "Because the numbers changed every day, we ran daily estimates starting in May. Have you seen The West Wing? It's honestly a lot like that."

Critical Clause #4

Lee didn't have a moment to relax; concerns about not having enough votes haunted him until the very last moment. If someone switched their vote, it could cause a domino effect and end in disaster. "We were constantly in touch with party opinion leaders," Lee said. "It wasn't until two, three days before the vote that we were finally sure that the bill had an opportunity to pass, though the final count might be close."

Yet, would a simple majority really be enough to appease the public? An important law like this needed an absolute majority in order to settle the issue once and for all. Lee explained, "If the bill passed by simple majority, then one day it could be overturned by simple majority. I reported our vote estimates to the president, premier, and other high level officials each day. Our goal was to eke out a supporting vote from at least half of the legislators to reach an absolute majority."

Phone calls plagued him night and day as Lee continued to work to secure the needed votes. "We used a multi-pronged strategy, or maybe," Lee laughingly added, "what many people refer to as emotional blackmail, to push politicians to be sure to vote for the bill. A single legislator might get a call from their close supporters, from Premier Su, or from a ministry director, all of which would urge them to vote." Both the supporting and opposing factions had already tried to rationally debate the issue for a long period of time. The final step was to resort to an emotional appeal.

If success is to be judged by the outcome, it seems this multi-pronged strategy not only worked but exceeded everyone's expectations. "The vote for the first clause was extremely tense, but we started to get excited when the votes were counted and had over 70 votes, far more than we anticipated. Then, when the crucial fourth clause passed with an absolute majority, you could hear the crowd outside cheering. My Line chat notifications were lighting up. It was then we were finally certain it would pass." Specific vote numbers after that point were a blur to Lee; they had crossed the biggest hurdle, he could finally breathe.

In accordance with Judicial Yuan Interpretation No.748 and this Act, a union, as stated in Article 2, shall be effected in writing, which requires the signatures of at least two witnesses, and by marriage registration at the Household Administration Bureau.
—Article Four of the Act for Implementation of J.Y. Interpretation No. 748

The word "marriage" is a controversial word to some people, so it was unclear if clauses four and seven, which explicitly use the word marriage, could pass. Supporters of the bill were highly concerned by the wording, but Premier Su continued to insist that the law must use the word marriage. Lee recounted, "There were still a few different versions of the law being debated in the Executive Yuan. The primary disagreement at the time was whether or not the law should use the word marriage." Lee repeated Premier Su's argument who said that "In 1979 I defended those convicted in the pro-democracy Kaohsiung Incident, and ever since, I have dedicated my life to equal rights for all. They want us to use the word marriage, why can't we give them that?"

Premier Su's argument persuaded his team of advisors, thus finalizing their stance on the wording of the law. "I was really moved by Premier Su," reflected Lee. "He wasn't making a showy, sensational speech to the public, he was sincerely expressing his personal values with a few political advisors.

Do we have to consider how this will affect our own candidates' elections? Of course we do. But there are some things that are more important." Lee thought back to Premier Su's work in the Kaohsiung Incident and expressed admiration: "When the first defence team for those convicted was arrested, Premier Su was willing to step up and join the second defense team. If he had only considered strategic advantage, he wouldn't have done so."

The Decade-Long Road to Marriage Equality: A DPP Advisor's Perspective

In Lee's 10 year career as a political advisor, he served both Premier Su Tseng-chang and President Tsai Ing-wen. It was during Su's campaign for Taipei mayor in 2010 that Lee first became involved in furthering LGBT rights. Su's campaign understood that Taipei City was relatively more progressive and felt he could declare his position on LGBT rights. For this reason, a supporter of the LGBT community, voice actor Francis Chia Pei Te, recommended Su participate in the annual pride parade.

"At the time, there weren't many politicians that were openly supportive of the LGBT community. Su was one of the few," said Lee. "Despite this, the pride parade did not want him there. Perhaps they weren't clear on his position and just thought he wanted to steal their limelight." Afterall, up to that point all doors had been closed to the LGBT community; never could anyone have imagined that Taiwan would become the first country in Asia to legalize same-sex marriage.

Advisors like Lee, however, were a bit more optimistic. "We could see that Taiwan should start working on relevant legislation. So we looked for how to create measures that could help grant same-sex couples rights without needing to amend the law. An example of this is something like the civil partnership registrations offered by individual cities. Honestly, even though legalized same-sex marriage was something we talked about often, we never imagined it would come to pass in 2019."

According to Lee, the DPP and activist organizations have a complicated relationship which can be traced back to the 2000 presidential election. In 2000, DPP President Chen Shui-bian was elected, marking the first time a political party other than the KMT was to hold executive power. President Chen's successful campaign was largely due to activist organizations, but their trust in him wore down over his controversial eight years in office. Lee stated, "Around 2008-2010, the DPP lost a lot of support from social activists. On top of that, the DPP was no longer the majority party and became rather powerless." According to Lee, over the years, politicians such as Premier Su and President Tsai Ing-Wen have expressed unwavering support of the LGBT community, but different political and historical contexts have led to this support being interpreted differently.

One example, stated Lee, was the 2016 election. "President Tsai expressed her support for same-sex marriage when campaigning. But after assuming office in 2017, she was criticized by LGBT organizations for not doing enough and for moving too slow. In actuality, the issue was that legislators were caught up in the debate over whether to amend the civil code or enact new legislation. There was resistance to new legislation because it was seen by many as discriminatory by being separate; what we didn't realize at the time was that it was the option more people would be willing to swallow."

Unfortunately, the ideal solution and the politically-calculated one do not always align. Lee admitted, "I was a part of the camp wanting to amend the civil code, but I was also very aware that the only viable option, politically at least, was separate legislation." He continued, "We didn't realize it at the time, but in hindsight, I think where we are today is a product of collective wisdom: the grand justices ruled the rights of same-sex couples must be protected, the public decided civil code should not be changed, and so ultimately we ended up with separate legislation. This legislation is a collective product of the legal system, political administration, and public opinion."

Though the Act for Implementation of Judicial Yuan Interpretation No. 748 may not be ideal, it is the culmination of the work of many parties and serves as an incremental step in the fight for equal rights.

The Sun Continues to Rise

A pivotal decision during the lawmaking process was naming the legislation. In May 2017, Judicial Yuan Interpretation No. 748 established that the current civil code was unconstitutional and set May 2019 as the deadline to resolve this violation. By February 2019, with the deadline inching ever nearer, lawmakers needed to complete the deliberation process but were stuck on what to name the law. "We discussed several names including 'The Same-Sex Partnership Act,' which LGBT organizations were against," said Lee, "and 'The Same-Sex Marriage Act,' which religious organizations were against."

Liu Chien-Sin, who was Deputy Secretary-General to the President at the time and at the time of this interview was Secretary-General of the Examination Yuan, worked with several advisors on the matter, racking their brains for a solution. Finally, Lee said, "Deputy Secretary-General Liu, who went to graduate school in the U.S., had a burst of inspiration. Why not use the U.S. standard format for law names: "Article No. + Implementation Act"? This format would not be particularly unusual, as it is similar to Taiwan's Act to Implement the ICCPR and the ICESCR."

Everyone held their breath as they waited to see how officials and key organization leaders reacted to this potential solution. Lee asked Jennifer Lu, a prominent LGBT rights advocate, to discreetly find out what key LGBT organizations thought of the title. "It turned out not only were they okay with it, they didn't think it was discriminatory, so we had a bit more confidence. We also asked

religious organizations, and they felt that it was acceptable since it did not have the word 'marriage.'"

It was thus that the Executive Yuan made history by boldly proposing this neutrally-named law. Lee believes, "This really gave LGBT organizations a shot in the arm. Even though the DPP lost big in the 2018 midterms, they were willing to propose separate legislation that was very similar in content and spirit to the civil code. In doing so, the law name would remind people of the supreme court ruling. A ruling by those who best understand the law, those who enjoy the highest degree of public trust, the grand justices." The government and activist groups finally found common ground and a mutual goal. They were able to come together to make adjustments, compromises, and corrections, providing a future model for government-activist cooperation.

Once the bill was named, political advisors such as Lee immediately set to work trying to educate the public about the new law. They contacted the media, created online guides, and asked Premier Su to record a video. The goal was, Lee said, that "We wanted everyone to see that this law passing would not change life in Taiwan. The sun would continue to rise. Fathers would still be called father, mothers would still be called mother. People would continue to have children. Sons that had always liked women would not suddenly like men. Those who had always liked men would continue to like men. Those who had always liked women would continue to like women. We were only granting rights that should have been granted in the first place."

The media campaign may have been complete, but the work of the advisors did not end there. After the third reading of the law passed, they had to have the Executive Yuan look over the marriage registration form from the Department of Civil Affairs to ensure that there was no discriminatory wording. No detail could be overlooked.

Lee has retired from his position as political advisor; he has moved to Kaohsiung to serve as Board Chairman for iPass. Yet, when asked to recall his role in the fight for human rights, he appears to be young, excited, invigorated. When asked if he misses it, he laughed and said, "I'm somewhat nostalgic. But two years ago, when the third reading passed, I went back to the Executive Yuan and told Premier Su that I had reached the peak of my career as an advisor and could now step down. I told him since this battle was over, I could leave without any regrets"

Lee may or may not return as a political advisor some day, but either way, his contributions in the fight to legalize same-sex marriage have already been enshrined in history.

....

Q & A

What does equality mean?

Equality means that everyone has the same rights. I often tell my children not to discriminate or bully others because we are all the same.

What does normal mean?

There's no need to define who is normal because it's all relative. It's only if we label ourselves as normal that we imply that there are others who are not normal.

....

——————————

Joseph Chang

* Please turn to page 160 for Chinese version

· Joseph Chang (Minister of True Light Gospel Church)

Inside the True Light Gospel Church, natural light pours through the frosted glass on which hangs a large cross, softening the solemn atmosphere. Pastor Joseph Chang peacefully strolls forward, smiling as he holds up a rainbow flag. The cross and the pride flag, the symbols of two communities with deep-seated conflict, are together at last, illustrating the progress Chang has made in his many years of work to bridge the divide between Christian and LGBT groups.

Chang grew up in a family of pastors. At 15, he considered himself a devout Christian, but when he was 18 he developed feelings for a fellow male believer at church camp and felt deeply ashamed. The two of them prayed for repentance. When he was 21, he wrote a heartfelt seven page letter to his parents in which he confessed he was gay. From that moment on, he went forth embracing both his religious identity and his sexual orientation. But this path turned out to be much more difficult than he anticipated.

The Ordination: Don't Ask, Don't Tell

Chang entered seminary determined to become a pastor, but his goal was nearly derailed by a number of anonymous letters sent to the seminary and church where he interned. These letters revealed Chang's sexual orientation and pressured the seminary to expel him. Thinking back on this experience, Chang softly said, "That experience was a wake-up call. It made me question whether or not I could really be a pastor. I was worried about what would happen if more people were aware of my sexuality. I wasn't sure if I would be able to graduate or get a church assignment." But it was too late, Pandora's box had been opened and what was once hidden inside had been exposed.

At first, Chang was so furious that he wanted to publicly come out but was dissuaded from doing so by several friends. Over time, the incident slowly faded. Chang said that in light of the letters, "A respected pastor recommended that I shouldn't look for a position in a church. If I was assigned to a congregation, parishioners would be sure to ask about my relationship status. And, at the time, I was living with my partner; people would talk." Instead, Chang chose to work for several years at the Presbyterian Church in Taiwan in a different capacity. But Chang wouldn't rest for long, and in 2007, he decided to start the process to become an ordained pastor, during which rumors flew once more.

"I heard that the committee discussed whether or not someone who is gay can be a pastor," recalled Chang. "Many people were opposed to the idea. Ultimately though, because nobody had ever directly asked me about my sexuality and I hadn't publicly come out, the committee approved my ordination. Fortunately, there were several pastors involved in the process who were supportive of the LGBT community. I'm very grateful they were willing to lobby for me."

At the time, the approach of the Taiwan Presbyterian Church was similar to that of the Clinton administration's policy on LGBT military members, "Don't Ask, Don't Tell." Those who were gay thus needed to know how to be discreet. The ordination ordeal forced Chang to realize that if he were to stay in the Presbyterian Church, he would have to pay a price: he "would have to be a deeply-closeted pastor."

It was for this reason that Chang decided to found an inclusive church that welcomes everyone regardless of whether they are gay, transgender, or straight. To him, everyone deserves to be loved by God. Ten years later, he successfully stands at the front of True Light Gospel Church before parishioners of all genders, sexualities, and a number of heterosexual families who wanted to be part of a church that embraces diversity.

To this end, the church has begun providing gender equity education for the children. Chang hopes even the church's youngest parishioners will be able to go forth and sow seeds of respect and tolerance throughout

society. "The children are raised from a young age to respect differences," said Chang, "including respecting people such as our transgender parishioners. At first the children might be unsure whether to address them as Ms., Mr., Aunt, or Uncle, but they soon get used to it. The parents of our congregation are also very helpful. There are many schools with strongly conservative PTAs, but when our parents are a part of these groups, they can help to start a dialogue." This strategy was a lesson Chang learned during the marriage equality movement.

No One is Perfect

Chang used to get upset with those opposed to the LGBT community, but the marriage equality movement forced him to learn how to communicate with people from many different walks of life. During the process, he realized he had built up a lot of resentment over the years. "I'm rather reserved, I suppress my emotions, but it still impacts my physical and mental wellbeing. It got to a point where I realized I couldn't go on like that."

He decided to try to empathize and understand the conservative faction's viewpoint. "I used to think that they were just stuck in their ways, homophobic, not exposed to any new ideas, but I realized this wasn't necessarily true." Chang explained, it may be that these people are "under pressure from their family, their social sphere, or impacted by a past experience." Putting aside his judgment, Chang admitted to himself that we are all human, no one is perfect.

"They are imperfect as am I. So first, I try to accept who they are and who I am. Then, I try to find common ground where we can begin the discussion. If they are firmly opposed, I just try to find a way to get along."

Chang believes that even if two people have opinions on the opposite ends of the spectrum, they shouldn't cut ties. "I used to be very upset with family members who were unaccepting.

But then I thought back to what I've lost in the past because of my own beliefs, and I realized that they may be afraid of what they will lose by changing their beliefs." Changing one's beliefs is difficult enough, it is even more difficult if there is a risk of losing power or privilege as a result. If a relationship between two disagreeing parties is maintained, however, one day an opportunity to have a meaningful discussion may arise.

As the marriage equality movement gained steam, so did the opposition, whose core driver consisted of conservative Christian groups. There was a period of time where the LGBT community saw Christianity as a cult. At the same time, the conservative Christians said the LGBT community was calling for sexual liberation and engaged in debauchery. This made Chang very sad: "As someone who is Christian and LGBT, I was stuck in the middle. I thought about my own identities and how I reconciled the two; I realized relationships were key." For instance, those that are LGBT and accepting of Christians probably have Christian friends, and those who are Christian and accepting of the LGBT community probably have LGBT friends. Chang explained, "Christianity teaches that all relationships, whether between two people or between a person and God, are based on love. Focusing on the relationship can help us to find a balance and understand one another."

Is Homosexuality Really a Sin?

Many are probably questioning that if Christianity is really based on love and tolerance, as Chang repeatedly said, then why do Christians make up such a large proportion of those opposed to the LGBT community? And why do they insist that the Bible condemns homosexuality?

Leviticus 20:13: If a man lies with a male as he lies with a woman, both of them have committed an abomination. They shall surely be put to death. Their blood shall be upon them. *(The New King James Version)*

According to Chang, this answer lies in how different sects interpret the Bible. "Honestly, this is a tough issue. The conservative faction takes a literal approach to what is written. The progressive faction believes that the social and historical context in which the Bible was written must be considered. One example I talk about a lot is that the Bible used to be used to suppress women and support slavery, but we no longer accept these interpretations anymore." Debates around biblical interpretation have always existed, and time is needed for interpretations to shift. A number of churches in Europe and the United States have spent two to three decades making the shift from preaching homosexuality is a sin to performing same-sex marriages. It isn't impossible for a conservative church to make this transition, but it is a matter of time.

According to Chang, "The Bible provides the best insight into understanding God's plans and designs, but it requires human interpretation. Many people fixate on what the Bible literally says, forgetting that there's more to Christianity. What we believe in is Jesus." In addition to a fundamental belief in Jesus, mainstream religions require a strong organization to thrive. Chang believes that oftentimes some of these issues are rooted in the organization, not the religious doctrine. "While ethics, social norms, church organization, and biblical authority should be of secondary importance to biblical teachings, many pastors feel that any change to these aspects may impact their authority or position." According to Chang, for many religious officials, religion is their entire world. When they realize that their voice has been challenged by something they are unable to understand, it's only natural for them to be scared. He argues, this is unrelated to religion, rather, it's human.

An Imperfect but Important Shift

Together with the Marriage Equality Coalition, Chang threw himself into the marriage equality movement. In 2016, he stood among the 250,000 supporters at a concert in support of marriage equality held on Ketagalan Boulevard. It was here that he was moved to find it was no longer just the LGBT community who were involved in the fight for equal rights. In the wake of the major defeat of the 2018 referendum, Chang held classes on spiritual growth and stress management to help the community heal. Finally in 2019, he stood among the crowd outside of the Legislative Yuan to witness the historical moment marriage equality was realized. He prayed that from that point on this new law will bring change to the church.

Some change, Chang said, has already begun. "I find that many Christians now understand that we cannot force everyone to live in accordance with Christian teachings. There are some that do not support gay marriage, but they choose not to vehemently oppose it or not to get involved in countermovements. They believe that they shouldn't prevent a group of people from fighting for equal rights just because of their own religious beliefs." Though the law may not be perfect yet, it is an important step forward in the learning process.

In the future, Chang hopes all churches will be willing to perform same-sex marriage ceremonies. He further hopes that those who are publicly out will be able to continue to serve as pastors.

Pictures of Chang and his partner on Instagram show them cutting a birthday cake, enjoying a lavish meal of steak and red wine, and wearing matching down jackets on a trip abroad. It's so ordinary, it's beautiful. Chang is a gay man, a pastor, and a husband. And what's wrong with that? To Chang, everyone should have the freedom to be who they are, and everyone is deserving of love.

....

Q & A

How do you define equality?

Equality is treating all life created by God with kindness, not just people but plants and animals too.

What is love?

Love is loving others as you love yourself. We must be empathetic and think about how we want others to treat us. Then, we should treat them in kind.

What does normal mean?

Diversity is normal. We are all unique just as each person's fingerprints are unique. Normal means accepting the world's many different people.

....

Mama Kuo

* Please turn to page 168 for Chinese version

· Georgia Kuo (Mama Kuo) (Founder of the Loving Parents of LGBT Association)

Clad in full rainbow gear, a woman everyone fondly calls "Mama Kuo" sat down and frankly asked, "Oh man, I have something to say to you all that might be a bit inappropriate. Is that okay?" After getting approval, every ten minutes or so Mama Kuo urged, "My LGBT friends, go get married already!"

"Inappropriate" turned out to be code for Mama Kuo planning on nagging all LGBT singles to pick up their pace towards the altar.

Mama Kuo is the founder of Loving Parents of LGBT. From its founding in 2011 to date, she proudly reported, every case they have assisted with has been successful. The association is made of a group of parents whose reaction to their children coming out was to fearfully move into the closet themselves. Now, as a part of Loving Parents of LGBT, they are best equipped to understand the reactions of parents of LGBT children and to help encourage these children to communicate with their families.

It's a Diverse World

Mama Kuo's own story began when her daughter ran away at 15 years old, leaving a note to her parents in which she came out. Mama Kuo was terrified. She immediately called her daughter and said, "No matter whether you like boys or girls, we love you. Come home!" Thinking back to her reaction, she jokingly said, "I had to say something comforting, or I might scare her away."

When many parents first find out their child is gay, they don't dare voice their own anxiety. Mama Kuo's reaction was to search for information online; together with her husband, she read several English resources. "At first we just wanted to know how to comfort her. We were worried; she was only 15. We didn't understand if this was something that might change as she got older." Despite her confusion, Mama Kuo was proactive about bettering her understanding, and, in 2004, joined the Taiwan Tongzhi Hotline Association. "Hotline really opened my eyes. Bears, twinks, pups, I had no idea the LGBT community was so diverse," she said gaily.

But no matter the community, the love is the same. Motherly love pushed Mama Kuo to learn more about the LGBT community than even her own child did. "I asked her what type of lesbian she was. A stone butch? A dandy butch? I would poke fun at her and say that she didn't seem to fit any of the labels, that she was somewhere in between."

Precisely because Mama Kuo clearly expressed interest, her daughter was willing to talk to her mother about her love life on campus. Mama Kuo explained, "a lot of girls liked her because she was quite handsome. She would even end up with arguments with girls if she couldn't find time in her schedule for them." With a laugh, Mama Kuo said her daughter "really needed to manage her time."

Serving as her daughter's personal relationship expert, mother and daughter had many in-depth conversations. So when a teacher tried to disclose to her that daughter was dating girls, Mama Kuo was ready to quash the discussion. "Her teacher was very worried. She said that my daughter went to sleep over at an older girl's house. The teachers seemed to think it was a huge deal. But I told her in my six years living in school dorms, we would leave campus for sleepovers all the time."

Mama Kuo expressed she sometimes worries her overwhelming motherly love needs to be brought in check, otherwise her daughter might think she's too needy. Perhaps as a result of this love, it was actually Mama Kuo who dove into learning more about different gender identities before her own daughter did. In the process, Mama Kuo realized her daughter might actually be transgender.

Finding the Answers Along the Way

From here on, we should refer to Mama Kuo's child as her son.

"Many people have asked me how he came to identify as transgender. I think it's because our family always recognized gender as a broad spectrum, and we asked him to reflect on his preferred expression. We asked a lot of questions and looked for the answers along the way."

"I knew he didn't like his chest, and so we started to look at options for breast reduction surgery." Mama Kuo's son started to think about surgery when he was in college, which proved to be challenging for her to accept. The source of contention was her own beliefs: "I believed that only the body given to us by the Lord is natural and that we should not harm this body. But then I thought about it, and I realized the Lord wouldn't prevent people from being happy. If someone changing their body helps them to accept themselves and, as a result, be happy, then why not?"

Clearly proud, Mama Kuo continued, "We supported our son throughout his transition. He decided not to take any hormones or go through voice therapy. Because he didn't try to hide the signs of a female body, he has many different physical characteristics. He didn't try to achieve a stereotypical male appearance. That's just who he is."

Mama Kuo embraced her son's transition as her own. Thinking back to her son's determination to be his authentic self and the process to get there, the pain of surgery, the recovery, and the permanent scars, tears rolled down her cheeks. It was in the spirit of a messenger of good news that Mama Kuo rushed to be the first to introduce her son to her neighbors. Instead of worrying about what they would think, she said that she "helped them see that the world has changed. I opened their eyes."

Now her son lives a peaceful life with his fiancee and is soon to be married. The two of them bought a house together long before same-sex marriage was legalized, and Mama Kuo is truly grateful that she has been able to be there for each milestone in her son's life.

From Hiding to Helping

In addition to guiding her own child, Mama Kuo has watched over many individuals and their families during the coming out process. Accordingly, she fully appreciates the effort it takes to transition from hiding in the closet to helping others out of it.

Yet, Mama Kuo humbly sees her work as a learning process. "The Lord gave me a special child, and, in doing so, provided me with the opportunity to serve others. If it were otherwise, I might just be sitting at home everyday with nothing to do but laze about."

The past few years, Mama Kuo hasn't missed a single advocacy event or event for families. She says her most important job is to alleviate the worry, anger, and opposition of parents of LGBT children. The 2018 referendum had both LGBT rights advocacy groups and opposition groups in full throttle, and Mama Kuo ended up contracting Bell's palsy from the extreme stress. "That was a really awful experience. We were truly trying to campaign for every single vote, and I went to sleep each night thinking about how to convince people. I would think about if there was anything I could phrase better or if there was any way for us to improve so that we could have a productive dialogue, especially with the religious community."

These in person dialogues can be hurtful and sometimes unproductive. So it was only natural to be disappointed after the major defeat in the referendum, but as an adult role model, Mama Kuo put this aside and patiently answered many calls from young members of the LGBT community. "Young people hoped we could help them convince their parents to be accepting, the same parents who are maybe pastors or pastor's wives. Those conversations are often intense. They will pull out the bible to show you its teachings, and there are just some questions that you can't answer. I think the biggest difference between me and them is that I am the parent of an LGBT child and know many in the community, so when I talk to them, I tell stories of individual people while they tell the story of God."

When asked how she endured so many challenging months, she merely shrugged away the thought. "The road ahead is still quite long. While the marriage equality bill has finally passed, there's still so much to be done. There are many stories of successful, harmonious families that are inspiring. Most parents just want to understand but often...children underestimate their parents. I've seen many instances where the children think their parents won't understand, but when I join the conversation I see just how much the parents love their children. The issue is that they don't have the right resources. I find, if it's for their children, the majority of parents are willing to learn."

Even many highly capable, accomplished members of the LGBT community can suddenly lose the ability to express themselves when at home. To these individuals, Mama Kuo issued a reminder: "In addition to accepting oneself, parents need to be accepted as well. LGBT children must guide their parents forward with them. I'm just a common, average person. If it weren't for my child, I wouldn't have learned so much about the world. There are more parents who may also be destined to help others. Maybe their child's identity will allow them to go talk to the old woman on the street or the local gossip and help raise awareness among different groups in society."

Towards this goal, the Loving Parents of LGBT has relentlessly worked to build connections with key individuals. According to Mama Kuo this means "working hard to engage those who are straight, who are older, who are capable, who have power, who make the laws." Ultimately, if they can reach one person, the impact will continue to resonate. For instance, LGBT children may impact their parents who then impact their extended families, so Mama Kuo has continued to encourage those in the LGBT community to put themselves out there and let society know: we are here.

Get Married Already!

Since its founding, the Loving Parents of LGBT has had an unwavering mission—to help more parents be accepting of the LGBT community. "I once had someone say to me 'So-and-so's child is gay. It's really unfortunate.' I responded by asking if he even knew the mother because doesn't think it's unfortunate, she's actually very happy. Our society has always thought that someone being gay is a problem. We need them to see more positive examples of LGBT families."

Mama Kuo suddenly made another appeal for all LGBT singles to get married, citing the statistics. "There were 3,000 couples who got married the year the new same-sex marriage legislation passed (2019). In 2020, it was a

little more than 2,000 couples. Because of the Covid-19 pandemic, there may be even fewer in 2021. After all, those that had been waiting for legalization have already gotten married by now." She went around the room and individually asked everyone present why they hadn't gotten married yet before earnestly saying, "We need to create a positive culture around marriage and having children, too."

According to Mama Kuo, "The legalization of marriage equality has helped many parents to be more accepting of their child's LGBT identity. They are reassured by the fact that their children can get married. And it isn't only parents that need to better understand how the LGBT community lives and loves, society needs to see more happy LGBT families before we are able to push for more rights like adoption or access to assisted reproduction options." Mama Kuo hopes that the legalization of gay marriage will also serve to disrupt family gender roles. "There are many traditional expectations towards division of household labor, but these expectations aren't applicable to LGBT households, meaning it can be more equal. Each individual can be responsible for the household work they are best at. Wouldn't that be great if heterosexual couples did that as well?"

In her final appeal, Mama Kuo said, "People in the LGBT community never thought marriage was a possibility. We've overcome innumerable obstacles to get to this point. Don't be afraid to go even further, go get married already!"

....

Q&A

What is kindness?

"Kindness starts with living your life as best as possible and wishing the best for others as well. Everyone deserves to have a better life, and helping others to have a better life, even in a small way, can influence someone's beliefs."

What is love?

"Love is responsibility and patience. When in love, two people will have to compromise. These compromises are what lead to personal growth. As you spend time together, you will learn from the other person." Mama Kuo jokingly added, "Couples also train each other. For example, my husband is in charge of the cooking. I often tell him that he is in charge of my meals until we're 90."

Bonus; Mama Kuo's Guide to Coming Out

First of all, don't destroy your relationship with your parents! Don't think you can suddenly come out after not visiting or contacting them for years. Instead, follow the steps below:

Step 1: Describe when you first questioned your identity and how you felt.

Step 2: Tell them about the moment when you knew for sure.

Step 3: Share details about major moments related to your identity, your past partners, and LGBT events you have taken part in.

Step 4: Tell them about your current relationship. (Recommendation: try to do this when you have a partner, a breakup is not a great time.)

Step 5: Tell them about your hopes for your future. Who do you want to spend your life with? Do you want to have pets? Children? Parents are most concerned that you won't have a family of your own. Coming out is not a science, and your parents might need some time before being able to understand. Wait for them to catch up.

I hope this helps everyone to be your happy, authentic self when with your loved ones.

....

Chen-Ling Wen

* Please turn to page 176 for Chinese version

· Chen-Ling Wen(Actress)

It may be pouring, but together we can hold up a rainbow against the storm.
We've made it this far, so I know we'll always be together. On today, the International Day Against Homophobia, Transphobia, and Biphobia, we are reminded everyone is created equal—we can get married ! Let's get married #Drenched #Needahotbath

In a picture posted to Instagram on May 17, 2019, Wen Chen-Ling stands outside Taiwan's Legislative Yuan, her arm over her friend Pipi Yao's shoulders. Though drenched, their hair plastered to their foreheads, the two radiant artists are beaming, their eyes crinkled at the corners. Wen first publicly expressed her support for marriage equality around 2016, and over the past three years, during the height of the marriage equality movement, she hasn't missed an opportunity to be involved. However, before throwing herself into the movement, she hadn't even realized equal rights for the LGBT community was considered an "issue."

What's Wrong with Same-Sex Attraction?

"At first, I was really optimistic," laughed Wen. "I'm a pisces, so maybe I was living in my own romantic fantasy of the world where everything is perfect. It was only after joining the protests and events that the truth finally dawned on me—apparently my beliefs were extremely different from certain segments of society." Wen, who was not yet 25 at the time, simply thought that a right as basic as marriage should easily be granted if enough people made themselves heard.

Wen never questioned her beliefs, even at an early age. By adolescence, she had already become accustomed to middle and high school female classmates having girlfriends.

She herself had been attracted to a girl at 17. "I didn't think that there was anything wrong with my sexual orientation," Wen reflected. "I've never been able to understand why some people think same-sex attraction is wrong or bad. What I think is weird are people that are unable to comprehend the existence of different sexualities." Wen went on to say that she is still sometimes attracted to friends of the same sex, "but the degree of attraction, and whether or not it becomes love, is another thing."

Perhaps this is why Wen used to be unable to understand people that hold anti-LGBT beliefs; in fact, the first time she saw someone holding a sign promoting anti-LGBT ideology she thought, "Does he know what his sign means?" However, after several years of experience and involvement, she started to rethink her assumptions. Wen realized that she "just naturally stood by what [she] thought was right, so maybe those that oppose the LGBT community were merely doing the same."

Looking back on the LGBT movement over the years, Wen expressed hope that progress will ultimately be achieved over time. "When the LGBT rights movement first began, I hadn't yet been born. If everyone does their best to assert their influence and communicate, then, over time, I know that things will get better." She thought back to her time studying abroad in Russia. When chatting with a Russian woman, Wen mentioned that she very much supports marriage equality. She didn't expect that the woman wouldn't understand. "The woman was already 19 years old but had never even seen a gay person on the streets of Moscow. When she told me that, I suddenly remembered how someone from college had told me if a gay person publicly displayed affection in Russia, they might be beaten."
Six months after returning home from studying abroad, she unexpectedly received a text message from the same woman. "She was very excited to tell me that she had just met her first gay man at a bar. She even talked to him." This is merely an example of what happens when a conservative society is cut off from

the rest of the world, meeting a gay person becomes a novel experience. Wen said, "I know I'm really lucky. Unlike this adult woman who had never had the chance to even see, let alone understand, the LGBT community, I grew up in an environment that provided me with the opportunity to do so." Wen believes this understanding is a blessing and is the reason that, for her, supporting LGBT rights was never even a question, it was the natural thing to do.

Tatakai! Keep Fighting!

In 2017, Wen won Best Leading Actress in a Mini-Series/TV Movie for The Last Verse at the 52nd Golden Bell Awards. When she took her award she said:

"I hope that before I turn 25 I will be able to witness the first gay marriage in Taiwan."

Though she is a public figure, Wen has never shied away from expressing her opinion, even when some of her audience might disagree with her. Wen believes, "Two people will always have their conflicts at first, even if it is someone you love dearly. It's just not possible to be completely on the same page from the start. You have to have discussions about your beliefs and opinions." Perhaps this is why she has not been concerned about losing fans due to her beliefs; in fact, she said, she hopes her beliefs help to open a discussion. "It's true that I have received a lot of critical messages from fans," Wen admitted." "I've even gotten a message that said, 'You must be a butch if you support LGBT rights so strongly, right?' But actually, messages like that make me want to support the cause even more."

Wen is very aware that those in the LGBT community not only receive similar hurtful messages each day, but that "those whose sexuality or gender is not affirmed by others are under constant attack from the moment they are born." This is why, she said, every time she receives a hurtful message, she becomes "even more sympathetic to those in the LGBT community who have to deal with the discriminating gaze of society each and every day."

It is this sympathy that carried Wen through the major blow the 2018 referendums served to the LGBT community. "That day, I went home and cried, but I quickly pulled myself together," said Wen. "If you just decide to accept the narrative that there's nothing you can do about the result, then it's easy to give up hope. Instead, I paid attention to how everyone was responding and reached out to friends that needed encouragement. I wanted everyone to believe that there was still a chance, that all was not lost, that we could still succeed." Despite the brave face she put on, Wen's courage to get back up strongly masked her own pain, but, she asked herself, "If I'm hurt, then how do those in the LGBT community feel?"

Though Wen acknowledged her experience may be different from that of those who identify as LGBT, she never felt like she was fighting for the rights of "others." "I don't see my rights as being separate from the LGBT community's rights. I see supporting marriage equality as supporting my own rights, the future rights of children, or the rights of people close to me that have not yet disclosed their identities to me."

Separate legislation, rather than amending existing civil code, may not be a perfect solution, but, like a rainbow after a storm, it is still worth celebrating. Wen knows that the fight is not yet over, but, as she said in her Instagram post, she wants to fight to the end. "I've recently become addicted to the series Attack on Titan, and I've learned the phrase: Tatakai, meaning continue to fight! After all, there are many aspects of society that are worth understanding, learning about, and even changing. I hope, as we do so, together we can continue to push forwards to a better tomorrow for all." Tatakai, if you fall down, get back up, and don't forget, none of us are alone.

Q&A

What does normal mean?

When there's something we don't understand, we might think someone isn't normal. But it's a big world, there are many different types of people. That's normal. We shouldn't try to change people just because we don't understand.

What is love?

Love is wanting those you love to be happy and to be willing to give selflessly without expecting anything in return.

What is kindness?

Adam Smith wrote that the greatest expression of kindness is following your heart and acting to benefit others. It's for these reasons that I support same-sex marriage.

Chih Chen Li

* Please turn to page 182 for Chinese version

· Chih Chen Li (Real Estate Agent; Former member of the Tainan Office for the Taiwan Equality Campaign)

There are many on the frontlines of the LGBT rights movement that don't make the headlines. Perhaps it was for this reason that Chih Chen Li was so surprised: "When I first saw my own name on the list of potential interviews for this photobook, I thought, Is this really a good idea?" Li, who had previously been a part of the Tainan Office of the Marriage Equality Coalition, thought about the decision for a long time but ultimately decided to accept the interview so that this book on the ups and downs of the LGBT rights movement would also include the work of those at the community-level.

New to the road, just recently haven gotten

her driver's license, Li took her time parallel parking upon arriving for her interview for which she sat at the tiny desk where she used to manage the Marriage Equality Coalition's advocacy work for Yunlin, Chiayi, and Tainan in 2018. Everything from recruiting volunteers to conducting training was done from this small space located in the office for the Tainan Sprout Association. Though young, 2018 was not the first time Li had taken on a leadership role; in fact, her background in the LGBT rights movement began early in college.

As she sat down for her interview in this familiar location, it became clear that Li has an air to her that immediately relaxes everyone around her. She carefully and thoroughly told us her story.

A Heterosexual's Political Awakening

Though she is now actively invested in political and social movements, Li didn't always sympathize with the LGBT community. "When I was younger," Li reflected, "I was actually extremely homophobic as a result of my father's views." Li's father was a well-known man in the area and conducted his business at home, meaning many of his neighbors and associates would come over often. Every time former President Ma Ying-jeou came up in their conversations, they would all scoff, "Homosexual. Sissy. Can't he say anything right?" But back then, few people understood gender temperament. Li gave an example: "In those days, Wu Qing-feng of the band Soda Green was in a juice advertisement where he would finish the bottle and make an 'Ahh' sound. When my father saw this ad, he would swear, 'Faggot,' and I would echo him. At that time, I never would have thought that I may know people who were LGBT. And since I was in Tainan, even if there were people I knew who were LGBT, they probably didn't dare to come out."

So it was not until the release of The Rebellious Daughter in 2001 that Li truly began to understand the LGBT community. The Rebellious Daughter, directed by I-Chen

Ko and adapted from the novel by Du Xiu-Lan, marked Taiwan's first television drama centered around lesbian characters, and soon after, in 2003, the novel Crystal Boys was similarly adapted into a epinonimous television drama and served as a record of the nature and politics around gay culture at the time. "Crystal Boys piqued my interest in the topic, and I even borrowed the novel." Li reflected that as a result, she "slowly started to understand what it meant for someone to be gay." Not long after, when Li started high school at an all-girls high school, she started to notice some of the older girls pair off into masculine and feminine couples. "But at that time, I just assumed that they would end up getting boyfriends later on," Li said.

The year Li graduated from high school was the same year Taiwan's Anti-Media Monopoly Movement issued its demands to protect the freedom of the press in Taiwan. Li was greatly inspired by the movement: "At that time, I was a huge fan of Huang Kuo-Chang (an important organizer of the movement). I would read a lot online about the issues....My major in college was related to public affairs and the professors in my department encouraged us to learn more about social issues like this." It was for this reason that Li was there on March 18, 2014, the day most physically and mentally devastating to the young people involved in the movement. As a witness to the epoch-marking change, that night, "Good night! Formosa!" by Fire Ex lulled Li, as well as all the other activists, to sleep, comforting them.

In 2015, the year before the presidential election, Taiwan's two major political parties observed a prelude to change as several minor political parties were established. Li thought back, "Jennifer Lu ran as a candidate for the [newly-formed] Social Democratic Party (SDP). I admired her from afar. I thought she was a superhero." Later, upon meeting Jhih-da Yang of the Green Party-SDP alliance and learning that he was gay, Li began to concern herself with the LGBT rights movement.

The Surprising Power of Social Media

The year of the presidential election, 2016, Li volunteered for Miao Poya's campaign team. "Later on, I also volunteered for Jhih-da Yang's campaign," she said. "The more I volunteered, the more invested I became. Jhih-da would even joke that I was like his office manager. Both Miao Poya and Jhih-da Yang were openly-gay candidates, and I wanted to do my part to contribute to the LGBT rights movement, so I would spend time trying to figure out how to best discuss their identities with the public." As she worked on the campaigns, Li was bound to witness the differential treatment of these candidates. She found that voters in southern Taiwan frequently abused the volunteers, sometimes even throwing flyers back in their faces.

However, at the same time, she found that it turned out that the support of a straight ally could have a real impact on other people's lives. Li said, "I was a part of the informal army of young, angry activists. I would share political rants on Facebook, so my Facebook friends gradually came to understand my political leanings. There were even people who told me that they felt brave enough to come out because of my posts and the changing social environment." Perhaps as a result, over time, Li's social circle changed too and is now composed of around 60% gay individuals.

By 2018, Tainan was due to host its third annual pride parade, "the Tainan Rainbow Pride Parade," explained Li. "But Tainan had never had any large-scale advocacy groups to organize it, so that year Jhih-da Yang served as the Event Coordinator and I was on the working team." Li threw herself into organizing, handling everything from the parade permits to the volunteer team. Then, also in 2018, it was confirmed there would be referendums hosted to determine Taiwan's future gay marriage law, so Jhih-da Yang introduced Li to Jennifer Lu and agreed to join the Marriage Equality Coalition at the Tainan local office.

Stirring Up Local Support

When Li first joined the Marriage Equality Coalition, the cities of Taichung, Tainan, and Kaohsiung each had someone in charge of their respective region. The elections that year were somewhat different because "the law had been amended so that those who were 18 years old could vote in the referendums." It was for this reason Li thought it would be good timing to start campaigning, but "traditional media outlets were not reporting on the referendums," sighed Li, "and so our work on the ground wasn't getting any attention."

But, after all, those who are trailblazers aim to speak up when no one else does. So as the referendum grew closer and closer, Li found herself with more and more to do: secure materials, reserve locations, talk to local candidates, coordinate with local interest groups, and this was all on top of continuing to expand the Marriage Equality Coalition.

"As the referendums drew nearer," Li reflected, "everyone became more and more anxious. I was acting as an official point of contact and so was frequently communicating with local volunteers. They felt they were receiving resources at a slower rate than places like Taipei. So I tried to help. At that time I went to Taipei every two weeks for meetings, and I would bring up this issue." Northern and Southern Taiwan are not only separated by distance, but the ability and resources of the two are also vastly different. Despite this, every time protests were arranged at Ketagalan Boulevard (a prominent protest location located near the Presidential Office in Taipei), a string of buses packed with supporters would ascend to Taipei from Taiwan's southern cities. Ultimately, if it weren't for the support of those living in Southern Taiwan, the 2016 concert in support of marriage equality never would have attracted 250,000 supporters.

Though they were in charge of preparation, setting up stalls, recruiting volunteers, hosting lectures, distributing information, and other advocacy work, "The strength of the Tainan office didn't come from the support of legislative groups," said Li. "Instead, our strength came from local LGBT-friendly businesses." The Tainan office garnered support from small businesses by talking to indie bookstores, coffee shops, restaurants, and local food stands and getting them to display rainbow flags in support of the LGBT community. In 2018 alone, their work recruited 300 businesses to support the movement in this way.

As a straight ally deeply involved in the LGBT rights movement, Li's sexuality was bound to be questioned. Sometimes it would even be from other LGBT volunteers who pushed her boundaries; in these instances, Li would worry about hurting them and didn't know how to directly turn them down. Other times her sexuality would be a point of conflict, like in one incident right before the referendum. That day a passerby turned away an Equality Campaign volunteer who was passing out flyers, and when Li went to check on them, they replied, "Yeah, well, the results of the referendum don't impact you straight people anyways."

"I understood she was upset, but I was really hurt by what she said," Li reflected. It was inevitable that emotions would run high before the referendum, so the Marriage Equality Coalition decided to establish a system in order to look after the mental health of those involved. Despite this, as the leader of a large group, Li still continued to put caring for everyone else ahead of caring for herself.

On the night of the 2018 referendum, the Equality Campaign's main office in Taipei held a video conference call with all of the local offices around the island, and, together, they watched the vote counting live. "Because of the referendum defeat, and the election of Han Kuo-Yu as Kaohsiung Mayor," Li explained, "everyone was very upset. All we could do was have a drink, play some guitar, and get through it together." Reflecting on that night, Li remembered hearing from those in the community about many friends who had stopped responding to messages. That night, she kept thinking to herself, "We've all worked so hard. We can't give up now. "

My Rotten Mother

Li is very articulate, and so, following in the footsteps of her mother, she took advantage of this skill and went back into real estate after the 2018 referendum work was complete. It was a way to allow her wounds to heal and start anew. While working for the LGBT rights movement, she had become more aware of the true meaning of what a "home" was, and when selling houses, she ran into gay couples finding their own homes. These ideas around the true meanings of "home" and "family" allowed Li to not only push for her ideals in the larger community but in her own family as well.

Due to her activist work, Li would occasionally receive gay publications in the mail. This, she said, may have caused her father to think she "was gay and still in the closet." Even so, they never talked about it in person, but through texting Li was able to point out fake news and politically incorrect statements to her father. Over time, her father's perspective began to change, he even voted in support of LGBT rights in the referendum.

As for her mother, she began to have some health problems during the year Li worked on the referendum. Her work prevented Li from spending a lot of time with her mother, and her mother found this upsetting. What made things worse was that Li's mother's church also preached anti-LGBT rhetoric. Still, the day before the referendum, Li's mother decided that although she would not support the LGBT community, she wouldn't vote against it either. Ultimately, she didn't cast a vote in the referendums.

But eventually there came a turning point— Jhih-da Yang's marriage. "Jhih-da and his partner had a really big wedding. My mother even helped me determine how much to give them for a wedding present...I'm really grateful to them. They showed my mother that there are LGBT people all around us." As Li's mother heard more and more mentions of the lives of Li's married LGBT friends, her reservations began to break down. And recently, together Li and her mother watched Cherry Magic! Thirty Years of Virginity Can Make You a Wizard?!, a yaoi television drama (a genre featuring gay male romantic relationships). While watching her mother asked, "Is this the male lead? Oh, wait, there's a second male lead? This character is kind of like Jhih-da, right?" Li laughed, "When she saw Yuichi Kurosawa caress Kiyoshi Adachi, she even said, 'Aww, they're so cute.' I think something like this is a teachable moment. She has become just as invested in the show as I am."

Those who enjoy yaoi often jokingly call themselves "rotten girls" from the Japanese, fujoshi. As Li's mother became more invested in the genre, or more rotten, she began to see gay relationships as normal, opening up the door for reconciliation between mother and daughter. To this end, Li credits to Jhih-da Yang, his partner Guo-fong Hong, the caress between Yuichi Kurosawa and Kiyoshi Adachi, and the growing influence of yaoi media for helping others everywhere see broader, more diverse possibilities for what a "family" can be.

....

ቦ]&Δ

What does normal mean?

As long as something doesn't cause harm to others, if you like it, then it is normal. It doesn't matter whether others like it or not.

What is love?

There are some family conflicts that don't necessarily need to be resolved. Like I mentioned, my mother and I fight nearly every day, but we continue to communicate. This is how we make it through to the next

day. Even though we fight, we both know that we'll wake up each morning and eat breakfast together. I suppose that is love.

....

THE EMERGENCY MEETINGS—REVISITED

* Please turn to page 190 for Chinese version

Though Taiwan's LGBT rights movement can first be traced back to the 1980s, it was the short period between 2016-2019 where great breakthroughs were finally made. To LGBT rights groups, it was those three years where the crucial battles were finally fought and won.

In 2019, Taiwan became the first country in Asia to recognize same-sex marriage. The driving force behind the same-sex marriage law, the Act for Implementation of Judicial Yuan Interpretation No. 748, were numerous LGBT rights groups and women's rights organizations who, in a show of democracy, had done their best to come to consensus and unite their forces. It was the Marriage Equality Coalition who brought these groups together, including the Taiwan Tongzhi Hotline Association, the Awakening Foundation, and the Taiwan LGBTQ Family Rights Advocacy among others. With the Marriage Equality Coalition at the head to coordinate the actions and resources of these groups, together they were able to finally break through the unending darkness that had plagued their work for years and reach daybreak.

The road to get there, however, was bumpy due to a constantly changing political landscape and social environment. Burdened with heavy expectations and pressure from both within and outside the organization, the Marriage Equality Coalition spent countless nights struggling to stay awake in emergency meetings that ran late into the night. Now, two years after the legalization of same-sex marriage, they have gathered together once again to reflect back on this perilous journey in one last emergency meeting.

Participants:

· Taiwan Equality Campaign (formerly the Marriage Equality Coalition): Jennifer Lu, Joyce Teng, Chang Shi Tsao, Yi Ting Kuo

· Taiwan Tongzhi Hotline Association: Leo Chih-Liu Peng (Deputy Secretary General), Sean Sih-Cheng Du(Director of Policy Advocacy)

· The Awakening Foundation: Chao-Yuan Tseng (Senior Research Fellow), Shih-fang Lin (Director)

· Taiwan LGBTQ Family Rights Advocacy: Shang Wen Tsai (Former Deputy Director)

· The Lobby Alliance for LGBT Human Rights: Cindy Su (CEO)

· GagaOOLala: Jay Lin (Founder)

Background 1

The successful creation of new legislation allowing for same-sex marriage in Taiwan is in large part due to the coordination and advocacy work of the Marriage Equality Coalition (formerly called the Marriage Equality Coalition). Though just how Marriage Equality Coalition came up with their organization name remains somewhat of a mystery, as a platform composed of many people, many different organizations, and full of love, it has proven a fitting title for an organization promoting marriage equality.

In the greater picture of things, the right to get married is only one of many LGBT rights. Despite this, LGBT and women's activist

groups from all areas proved willing to work together and find common ground in order to reach this end. But just how did they first come together?

Q: How did the Marriage Equality Coalition first decide to advocate for LGBT marriage rights? And how did the various organization members consolidate their resources?

Jennifer: Uhh, wait, how did we first decide to establish this group again?

Multiple people at once: I think it was because of Legislator Mei-Nu Yu, right?

Chao-Yuan: I'll explain. Joyce and I used to be aides for Legislator Mei-Nu Yu. I started in 2019...wait that's not right. [laughing]

Shang Wen: You're ready to go home aren't you?

Chao-Yuan⊠I was an aide for Legislator Yu between 2012-2015. Before and after that period, I worked at the Awakening Foundation. In 2013, the Taiwan Alliance to Promote Civil Partnership Rights (TAPCPR) had lobbied Legislator Li-Chiun Cheng to introduce a bill for same-sex marriage, and Legislator Yu co-sponsored the bill. But the bill never finished going through the Legislative Yuan before the session was over in 2015, meaning it would need to be reintroduced in the new session. Fortunately in 2016, shortly before the Marriage Equality Coalition was formed, Legislator Yu was elected to her second term. When the new session of the Legislative Yuan began in February 2016, Legislator Yu privately asked Legislator Cheng if she planned to sponsor the bill again and learned that Legislator Zheng had no such intentions because she was actually planning to accept a position as the next Minister of Culture. Since the 2013 version of the bill had been met with a lot of opposition from opponents of LGBT rights and would need numerous revisions, Yu took the opportunity to completely rewrite

the bill. But she realized if she were to do this herself, she would need to consult with LGBT organizations. That's when discussions about creating the Marriage Equality Coalition first began. At least, that's the short answer.

Shang Wen: Have you ever had a short answer to anything?

Jennifer: So Cindy and Jay, how did you come to join? Who invited you to that first meeting?

Cindy: I was also asked by Legislator Yu's campaign team.

Jay: I remember very clearly that you asked me, Jennifer, when we were both at the Queermosa Awards. Legislator Yu also asked if I was interested in committing to the cause.

Jennifer: Ohh, I remember that night now!

Jay: [Laughing] You might have had too much to drink that night.

Jennifer: True, I had quite a bit that night....We then wanted to collect donations online, so we had to come up with a name. Is that right?

Chao-Yuan: Right, we really started discussing names in order to collect donations. Before that point, any rallies we organized were jointly held by all of the groups involved.

Jennifer: But all of our organization names are so long. It took forever for me to read them all out at events, and it was far too long in writing. But organization names with words like "Resource Center" or "Alliance" sounded dull and overused. Then, around that time there was the incident where actor Darren Wang messed up his lines at the MAMA awards and accidentally said something about giving everyone a "big platform." [Translator's note: the abbreviated Mandarin for the Marriage Equality Coalition literally translates to "big platform."] The young guy in charge of our website said that because of this incident a lot of people were using the term "big platform" online, and we could get more hits by using it. And then we ended up actually using this name. [laughing]

Background 2

By the end of 2016, the Marriage Equality Coalition had united all of its member organizations, joint discussions with Representative Yu about the various provisions of the bill had been completed, and the timeline for introducing the bill was set for after the 2017 Lunar New Year. No one was in a rush to introduce the bill: societal opposition was fairly low, opposition groups hadn't issued any extreme statements or taken strong action, and President Tsai Ing-wen had made a campaign promise to support marriage equality.

What was not expected, however, was that Professor Jacques Picoux of National Taiwan University would die the day before the 2016 pride parade, shocking the community. The tragedy drew wide-spread attention to the issue of the rights of same-sex couples. It was around this same time that a newly elected Kuomintang (KMT) legislator, Yu-Jen Hsu, publicly announced his intentions to sponsor a marriage equality bill, putting pressure on the Democratic Progressive Party (DPP) to introduce their bill first.

Q: Originally, the plan was to introduce the bill to amend civil code in 2017. Why was this plan suddenly changed to 2016?

Chao-Yuan: At that time, we had mostly completed discussing the provisions of the bill, and Legislator Yu had coincidentally been assigned to be the head of the Judiciary and Organic Laws and Statutes Committee (JOLSC). But at that point we hadn't yet established our campaign strategy, there was no reason to rush.

Leo: The plan was originally to introduce the bill in 2017, but this really changed in light of Professor Picoux. It catalyzed things forward.

Sean: Yeah, and especially because it happened the day before the pride parade. And with President Tsai publicly promising to support same-sex marriage during her campaign, public opinion was in our favor.

Shih-fang: [Trying to speak into a broken microphone.]

Jennifer: Oh, Shih-fang, did you want to say something?

Shih-fang: Sorry, can you hear me now? I just remembered another factor. Legislator Hsu went on the television program PTS Talks and stated he was going to introduce his own bill. So we said to the DPP, "If you don't introduce a bill before the KMT does, it will reflect really poorly on the party."

Chao-Yuan: Right, because DPP President Tsai had made a campaign promise, putting the DPP under pressure to introduce the bill before Legislator Hsu. So Legislator Yu quickly lobbied a large number of cosponsors and then held a press conference to state she was officially introducing the legislation.

Leo: I remember around that time Legislator Yu met with us to discuss the decision, and we decided then and there to go for it.

Background 3

After Legislator Mei-Nu Yu introduced the bill, the Legislative Yuan's JOLSC convened on November 17, 2016 to commence deliberation procedures. That same day, conservative groups opposed to LGBT rights resorted to drastic measures: they took out an advertisement in the newspaper calling for protesters to assemble outside the Legislative Yuan where they fell to their knees pleading and tried to scale the walls of the building. There were even some protesters who used their connections with a political aide to sneak into the meeting chamber. Ultimately, Legislator Yu's personal safety was threatened by their extreme speech and actions, and she departed under security protection.

Watching from a distance were the member organizations of the Marriage Equality Coalition who had gathered at Cafe Philo to watch the live streaming of the committee meeting. They were shocked by the actions of the opposing faction; not only did they feel as though they had been unjustly attacked, they also felt terrible for how Legislator Yu had been treated. A good number of people shed tears. This incident destroyed any illusion they once had about the road ahead of them. As they removed their rose-tinted glasses, they realized that even with all of the advantages behind them—the public support of the president and positive public opinion polls—the road ahead would continue to be littered with hurdles.

Q: On November 17, 2016, while chairing the JOLSC meeting to deliberate the proposed legislation, Legislator Yu was met by strong opposition from anti-LGBT groups. How did you all react?

Jennifer: If I remember correctly, we had decided not to organize on the day of the deliberation. Wait...Joyce, why are you making that face? Do you not remember anything about that day?

Leo: I think everyone's going to think we're all having this discussion while totally drunk. [Explosive laughter]

Chao-Yuan: At that time, since Legislator Yu was chairing the committee, we decided to try to avoid provoking the opposition too much, so we decided against a rally.

Shih-fang: And the anti-LGBT groups hadn't done anything like this before. Even the rally at Ketagalan Boulevard on November 30, 2013 by the True Love Alliance couldn't compare.

Chao-Yuan: Right, we'd never seen them get on their knees and beg.

Sean: And at that time we thought that there was overall support for the bill. We didn't want to make it seem more controversial or stir up controversy by rallying. We wanted the government to feel confident that it would pass.

Leo: Yeah, so we didn't expect such an...extreme counterprotest.

Shih-fang: The government did feel it was a thorny issue. That's why we had agreed to try to stay discreet and let the bill pass quietly. It wasn't until later we realized that would be impossible. [laughing]

Jennifer: Where were we that day? Cafe Philo? Shang Wen was probably at work, right? Jay, were you there?

Shang Wen: What? I'm not always at work!

Jay: I took a group to film at the Legislative Yuan that day.

Chao-Yuan: Yes, we had booked the space to watch the live stream. We saw them charge into the Legislative Yuan and bang on the meeting hall door. They looked completely immune to reason and were screaming, "Mei-Nu Yu, don't do this to us!"

Cindy: Those of us at Cafe Philo were in constant contact with Legislator Yu's aides and Legislator Hsu. They let us know what was going on. We were terrified the opposition groups would charge into the meeting chamber and harm Legislator Yu; we hadn't expected them to resort to physical violence.

Shih-fang: That day we hadn't even expected

the opposition groups to rally. So things felt really chaotic when we started getting all these updates. On top of that, the internet in the basement of the cafe that day was super, super, slow! We kept asking what's happening now? Why can't we hear anything? [laughing]

Jennifer: Yeah and when the legislators tried to call us, we didn't have a good enough signal to answer. Both Legislator Yu and Jason (Legislator Hsu) called to ask if we would support public hearings, but we were firmly against them. After the committee meeting was forced to adjourn, the media kept asking us for a statement, so we decided to host a press conference in the space next to the Legislative Yuan's Research Building. We left Cafe Philo and inconspicuously made our way towards the Legislative Yuan. We went in the back door, because we were afraid if we ran into the opposition protestors, we would be attacked. That day a lot of people online were debating whether or not they should try to rush the Legislative Yuan. They felt the opposition had, so wondered why weren't we?

Shih-fang: Nobody ever hosts a press conference in that space. It was behind the Legislative Yuan's Research building at the intersection of Zhenjiang Street. But still a minister from the anti-LGBT faction ran over screaming at us. It was an insane day.

Jennifer: Oh yeah, what was her name again? I've forgotten. Socrates? Socralade? Something like that. [laughing]

Leo: Her name was Shindibola (忻底波拉). The point was she recognized us and screamed at us a lot.

Jennifer: How were you all feeling after that day? Do you all remember?

Chao-Yuan: A lot of us cried, right everyone? Be honest!

Leo: Looking back, I feel that we had misassessed the situation. We had no idea

the opposition would fight back so intensely. I guess it hurt because we had originally thought the bill could easily pass, but then we had to concede to two public hearings. It felt like we were being pushed around. And I actually saw Chao-Yuan crying!

Chao-Yuan: I remember you crying first!

Leo: Alright, alright, I admit I cried first. Happy?

Jennifer: The two of you are pretty stoic. I've never seen you cry!

Leo: Part of it was that I felt bad for Legislator Yu.

Cindy: Yeah, we were all really afraid the opposition would hurt her. They were acting so irrationally; it was scary. We were worried it would turn into an intense fight between the two factions.

Leo: And before this we had never seen anti-LGBT protestors resort to physical violence.

Jennifer: Probably because they don't dare touch someone who is gay. They probably think if they touch someone who is gay, they might become gay themselves. In past demonstrations, they had encircled those from the LGBT community before, surrounding them and not letting them move, but they had never scaled walls before!

Background 4

After that fateful day, the JOLSC had to hold two public forums before continuing deliberation, but the real impact was on the Marriage Equality Coalition who, after being an unwitting witness to the new tactics of the anti-LGBT rights faction, were now aware of what they were up against. In response, the Marriage Equality Coalition decided to hold frequent rallies but also do their best to avoid direct confrontation. This way, they could unite supporting factions and show the public that they may have lost a battle, but they would not lose the war.

Full of determination, the Marriage Equality Coalition began the fight against the anti-LGBT factions for road closure permits. If it was a date where it was remotely possible that the Legislative Yuan might review the bill, right before midnight, when the system opened, Chang Shi would be in front of his computer with a stack of IDs ready to use to book public assembly permits. Fingers flying, he would quickly apply for anything available around the Legislative Yuan—Qingdao East Road, Linsen South Road, Zhongshan South Road or Jinan Road—it didn't matter, TEC wanted them all.

Q: After the terrifying antics of the anti-LGBT factions, how did you determine your strategy going forward and plan your next steps?

Jennifer: Chang Shi joined us exactly for this reason. [Laughing] After some discussion, we decided that we wanted to organize rallies on any day when it was possible the bill would be deliberated. This meant we had to book any available spaces.

Shang Wen: Right, we decided we didn't want to confront the opposing faction head-on, but we would rally.

Chau Yuan: It really was because of their extreme actions on November 17 that we decided any future rallies on our part needed to be comparable. It simply wasn't enough to have support from legislators.

Chang Shi: It was around then that I was recruited. I was told that "going forward we may need to frequently mobilize supporters," but in the beginning, a lot of those involved in the mobilization work were not full time staff. We realized this would be an issue if our efforts were going to be continuous.

Shih-fang: [Microphone still malfunctioning.] Hello? Hello? Can you hear me? I remember us looking at the calendar and gauging which days it might be possible for the bill to be deliberated or read. [Laughing.] We decided we had to apply for permits for all of those days.

Joyce: The anti-LGBT rights groups rallied on December 3 at Ketagalan Boulevard, so we decided we would rally immediately following that. December 10 happened to be Human Rights Day and that's when we organized the concert that attracted 250,000 people.

Leo: So many people came because everyone was really upset after the anti-LGBT group's event.

Chang Shi: Our plan was that if they organized an event, we would organize one in the days immediately after. We wanted to avoid confrontation with them, so when we organized an event or rally we would also apply for permits for the surrounding areas. This meant if we rallied in front of the Legislative Yuan, we would also apply for permits to Qingdao East Road, Linsen South Road, Zhongshan South Road or Jinan Road. Each time we wanted to apply, I would be prepared with everyone's ID numbers on hand ready to register before anyone else could as soon as the system opened.

Jennifer: But organizing events is very expensive, small NGOs like us almost went under. Jay and Cindy helped us raise the money we needed.

Chang Shi: I remember when I printed out our budget and gave it to Jay and Cindy, they took one look at it and said they would find a way. Then, after the first fundraising event, the first 100,000 NTD came in.

Jennifer: We really relied on you two!

Sean: We had a lot of people helping us at that time. Even the opposition helped us somewhat with their media campaign. Not only did they spread a lot of rumors, they bought media advertisements, and promoted a ton of fake news. Even heterosexual individuals not involved in the movement thought their media campaign was ridiculous.

Jennifer: Jay, you were fundraising at that time. How did people respond to you?

Jay: I think everyone understood that LGBT organizations were completely determined to do their best. For fundraising, Cindy and I decided to first contact older couples that had LGBT children, because they were more likely to be able and willing to donate. We also contacted those in the entertainment industry who would be likely to have the means. Some weren't willing to donate publicly, but were still quite generous with their contributions. That first 100,000, 150,000 NTD goal was pretty easily met.

Background 5

By the last few months of 2016, rallies became far more frequent, and in May 2017, the Constitutional Court issued its interpretation stating that not allowing same-sex couples to get married was unconstitutional. Furthermore, the court set a deadline of two years in which to amend the law. If the law had not been amended within that period of time, then same-sex couples would be able to get married under the existing civil code. This was the first real victory for pro-LGBT groups in Taiwan to date. At first, most believed they would only need to worry about whether the provisions of the bill were comprehensive enough. No one could have predicted that the opposition groups would call for a referendum in 2018, causing the Marriage Equality Coalition to have to take up arms once more.

Originally, the Marriage Equality Coalition

had planned a campaign urging voters to cast "Three No's" on the referendum measures raised by the opposing faction. But this simple slogan could no longer be used once Councillor Miao Poya suddenly announced on Facebook that she was going to petition to get her own referendum on the ballot in support of LGBT rights.

Q: By early 2018 anti-LGBT rights groups had initiated their referendum against amending civil code to allow same-sex couples to marry. What were your considerations at that point? Why did you decide to respond by initiating a separate referendum in support of same-sex marriage?

Jennifer: Honestly, at first we only planned a campaign pushing for "Three No's" on the referendum vote, but then someone initiated a referendum in support of same-sex marriage….So we decided, uh, does anyone remember how we settled on our "Two Yeses, Three No's" strategy?

Sean: It was because of advice the Marriage Equality Coalition got from similar international organizations. The U.S. organization Freedom to Marry told us that when facing referendums, voters are confronted with a lot of information. Since this can be confusing for them, the best strategy is one that clearly tells them how to vote. Strategically, a campaign for "Three No's" would work, but then there were the other two initiatives raised so we had to change the slogan to "Two Yeses, Three No's."

Jennifer: Do you all remember how you felt at that point?

Leo: It was you who was most upset at that point! [Laughing] I remember you went and met with Miao Poya, right?

Jennifer: Yeah, I invited them to the Taiwan Tongzhi Hotline Association office to discuss with a few of us. Miao Poya had announced that she wanted to initiate a referendum measure on social media, and we hoped to convince her campaign to not go through with it. But Miao Poya and social media influencers like Wen Lang Dong said that they wanted to let the people decide.

Chao-Yuan: The opposing faction was highly concerned because the constitutional court had already issued its interpretation that favored LGBT rights. So they wanted to use the referendum to overturn this ruling. But, strategically, our side really only needed to wait for the Legislative Yuan to pass a bill or for the two year deadline to pass.

Jennifer: Right, that's why we felt that it was illogical to initiate an additional referendum in support of same-sex marriage. But I guess Miao Poya was just really passionate, and she had already posted on social media. Since she hadn't discussed it with us beforehand, we didn't really have an opportunity to intervene.

Shih-fang: In the end, for the sake of avoiding conflict, standing together, and because people would ask us, we helped collect petitions needed to get the measure on the ballot. After the two measures got on the ballot, we settled on the "Two Yeses, Three No's" slogan.

Jennifer: We weren't surprised by the referendum results. The poll results from mid-November were terrible. At the time, we questioned if they were accurate or not. [Laughing] We even consulted a political science professor at the time because everyone thought it wasn't possible. We discussed it for a while and ultimately decided not to publish the poll results.

Leo: We conducted three polls in total.

Jennifer: Poll results from July and September showed a 50/50 split. But the results of the last poll in November showed support had fallen 20%.

Leo: I think it was probably because the opposition was campaigning at a national scale.

Shih-fang: They had several 30-second television ads that got far more exposure than our own. And though we raised money for advertisements and promotions, they were often rejected by the television stations.

Shang Wen: Once we had booked time slots several months in advance, but when it got to October, the station chair decided to not allow the ad to run. And that was it.

Jennifer: Even our bus ads were turned down.

Sean: Once we were sure there would be referendums, we knew they were bound to have an emotional impact on LGBT individuals. We thought a lot about what we could do after the referendums were announced, like provide phone counseling.

Leo: After the referendum results were final, even my own mental health was affected. At that time, the Taiwan Tongzhi Hotline Association worked with several other LGBT organizations to host some events to support the community because a lot of people were really in a bad place.

Jennifer: That night, as soon as the votes were mostly counted, we started discussing. We knew that if we showed we were depressed and upset, the community would feel like things were hopeless. But, as activists, we had the responsibility to communicate that there was still hope and that we wouldn't give up.

Background 6

After being crushed in the referendum, and no longer able to amend civil code, the Marriage Equality Coalition tried to stay hopeful as they moved forward with their efforts in lobbying to ensure the provisions of the new legislation were as comprehensive as possible. Finally, on May 17, 2019, as the banging of the gavel echoed throughout the Legislative Yuan, the Act for Implementation of Judicial Yuan Interpretation No. 748 was officially passed. The crowd standing outside the Legislative Yuan, clad in ponchos against the pouring rain, embraced and cried tears of joy. Then suddenly, as if the sky had heard their joy and wanted to share in it, a rainbow emerged. In contrast to the emotional crowd, the Marriage Equality Coalition, who had perhaps been under the most pressure and taken on the greatest responsibility over the past three years, was businesslike and neutral in their reactions. That day, they were really more interested in finally getting a good night's sleep than celebrating, or so they thought. In actuality, it was just that they needed more time to truly appreciate the significance of it all, and as they returned to their everyday lives, small unsuspecting details helped them each realize just how great of a feat they had accomplished.

For Chang Shi, this realization came when he took part in a same-sex couple's wedding for the first time. Upon seeing his friend, their partner, and both sets of parents at the front of the wedding hall, Chang Shi became completely overwhelmed: "I realized I had actually changed their lives. I had changed Taiwan. It was awesome, beautiful."

As for Shang Wen, his years of effort taught him both the difficulty and importance of maintaining a willingness to communicate. He reflected, "I have to admit, a lot of the time I really didn't want to try to reason with the opposing faction. But as a representative of the Marriage Equality Coalition, I had to uphold our reputation and promote our positions. Looking back, I think this may be the biggest way in which I've grown."

Two years have now passed since the legalization of same-sex marriage, and over that time Shih-fang and Chao-Yuan have truly realized that if everyone is willing to contribute, even in a small way, anything is possible. Shih-fang explained, "Many people took it upon themselves to try to bring about societal change. For example, there were students of the constitutional court justices who decided to come out to them. The impacts of their actions were far-reaching, and I found it incredibly touching." Even Chao-Yuan, who had been involved in the women's rights movement for over ten years, had never seen such a high level of involvement in a social movement. She reflected, "I'd previously only seen organizations mutually supporting each other in this way. This was a really inspiring experience that taught me a lot. What a social movement has to ask themselves is just how can we get more people willing to contribute?"

Jay, who was key to fundraising, feels he personally witnessed the power of a democratic society and found that "It turns out if you are willing to speak out, you actually can change history." Lastly, as a fitting ending to this treacherous yet spectacular journey, Jennifer concluded, "Everything is possible. If we can get through this, we can get through anything."

It's true. Together, we did it. Thank you to the Marriage Equality Coalition, and thank you to everyone who bravely joined us in our journey to equality.

mark 166

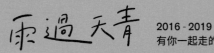 2016 - 2019
有你一起走的婚姻平權攝影故事書

作　　者	社團法人台灣彩虹平權大平台協會
專案管理	呂欣潔、郭宜婷
專案執行	鄧筑媛、陳乃嘉
內文撰寫	黃銘彰、李姿穎、陳芷儀
英文翻譯	Amanda Barrow
中文翻譯	巫靜文
影像監修	林科呈
攝影授權	Aki YJ Chen、B、BARBARIANIMAGE 野人寫真、cyuliu、DSX、Jim Wu、Ivy、Kerry C. Yang、Louis OuYang、Tigetx 虎哥、Webber 毛、大樹影像、幻想之龍、李懷仁、沃草、余孟翰、吳奕男、侯如寬、莊皓然、湯翊苂、郭宜婷、陳臆婷、捷安、麥麥、簡穎珣、韓宜臻、鐘聖雄
責任編輯	林盈志
企劃編輯	劉玟苓
校　　對	呂佳真
裝幀設計	謝捲子

本書圖片皆為彩虹平權大平台、活動攝影志工及夥伴提供。
若對圖片使用有疑問，請聯絡彩虹平權大平台：（02）2365-0791

出版者：大塊文化出版股份有限公司
105022 台北市松山區南京東路四段 25 號 11 樓
www.locuspublishing.com
讀者服務專線：0800-006689
TEL：(02)87123898　FAX：(02)87123897
郵撥帳號：18955675　戶名：大塊文化出版股份有限公司
法律顧問：董安丹律師、顧慕堯律師 版權所有 翻印必究

總經銷：大和書報圖書股份有限公司
新北市新莊區五工五路 2 號
TEL：(02) 89902588 FAX：(02) 22901658

初版一刷：2021 年 10 月
定價：新台幣 650 元
ISBN：978-986-0777-45-1
All rights reserved. Printed in Taiwan.　　　　特別感謝 Emoji 提供：Designed by rawpixel.com / Freepik

雨過天青：2016-2019 有你一起走的婚姻平權攝
影故事書 = The Calm after the Storm./ 社團法人
台灣彩虹平權大平台協會作 . -- 初版 . -- 臺北市：
大塊文化出版股份有限公司 ,2021.10
　面；　公分 . -- (mark ; 166)
ISBN 978-986-0777-45-1(精裝)
1. 同性婚 2. 同性戀 3. 社會運動 4. 臺灣
544.329　　　110014753